P.O.W.E.R. MOMS 3.0

Persevere. Overcome. Win. Empower. Restore.

Stories of Triumph Through the Lenses of Powerful Women of Faith

Authors:
Dr. Sherrie Walton
Kineta Lewis-Harrison
Araceli Avionn
Dr. Linda Bell-Robinson
Alessi Johnson
Nkia Haughton
Sandra Heard
Eureka Turner-Patton
Shannon Gooden

Walton Publishing House

Copyright © 2020 by Dr. Sherrie Walton, POWER Moms

All rights reserved. In accordance with the U.S. Copyright Act of 1976, the scanning, uploading and electronic sharing of any part of the book without the permission of the publisher constitute unlawful piracy and theft of the author's intellectual property. If you would like to use material from the book (other than for review purposes), prior written permission must be obtained by contacting the publisher at admin@iamsherriewalton.com. Reviewers may quote brief passages in reviews.

Walton Publishing House

Houston, Texas

www.waltonpublishinghouse.com

Printed in the United States of America

Disclaimer: The advice found within may not be suitable for every individual. This work is purchased with the understanding that neither the author nor the publisher, are held responsible for any results. Neither author nor publisher assumes responsibility for errors, omissions or contrary interpretations of the subject matter herein. Any perceived disparagement of an individual or organization is misinterpretation.

Brand and product names mentioned are trademarks that belong solely to their respective owners.

Library of Congress Cataloging-in-Publication Data under ISBN:

Paperback: 978-1-953993-00-7

Digital: 978-1-953993-01-4

Hardback: 978-1-953993-02-1

Table of Contents

Chapter One: A Purpose-Full Life 4
Dr. Sherrie Walton

Chapter Two: Breaking Free from Your Comfort Zone to Live Your Best Life 22
Kineta Lewis-Harrison

Chapter Three: Finding Your Invisible Strength 40
Araceli Avionn

Chapter Four: Living Life on Your Own Terms 56
Dr. Linda Bell-Robinson

Chapter Five: She Was Born: The Fibers that Created Her Being 72
Alessi Johnson

Chapter Six: From Trauma to Triumph 88
Nkia Haughton

Chapter Seven: The Power of Forgiveness: The Key that Unlocks the Door to Freedom 104
Sandra Heard

Chapter Eight: A Confident Woman 120
Eureka Turner-Patton

Chapter Nine: Shift Your Mindset to Abundance 136
Shannon Gooden

About the Power Moms 153

Hello Beautiful!

I can't wait for you to dive into the stories in the pages of this book. I must say, the P.O.W.E.R. Moms series is one that my heart is deeply connected to. I have a desire to align with women, especially mothers, that despite the obstacles that life throws their way, continues to fight, and thrive to be the woman of God she has been created to be. It's not always easy to get up after you have been knocked down, trust me I know, I have been knocked down quite a few times. But a winner keeps trying and eventually after you have put one foot in front of the other, you realize you have reached your goal.

This book is filled with tools you can utilize to help you elevate your life, career, faith and family to the next level. As you read through the pages, I want you to take a moment to see yourself through the lenses of each woman telling her story. You will laugh, cry and high-five the authors, and at the end you will realize that we are more alike than we are different. We are in a pivotal time in our world, where only the strong will survive. God has not only given you the instructions in His Word, but He wants you to connect with leaders, encouragers, motivators, teachers and Kingdom women that believe in you and want to see you succeed. You have found your safe place here, so go ahead and embrace the journey with the women revealed throughout the pages of this book.

P.O.W.E.R. Moms 3.0, Stories of Triumph Through the Lenses of Powerful Women of Faith, will challenge you to look at yourself and evaluate your life. It will also create an atmosphere for you to celebrate yourself for the amazing person that you are and the milestones you have reached. You are in the right place, at the right time and you will be blessed.

Grab your favorite cup of coffee, or tea, pull your hair back, relax and get ready to enjoy!

Kingdom Blessings,

H.E. Dr. Sherrie Walton

Dr. Sherrie Walton

What are the three words that best describe you?

Caring, Unstoppable, and Warrior.

What is the biggest challenge you've ever faced in life?

Wow, where do I begin. The biggest challenge I have ever faced was overcoming the "Imposter Syndrome" after my business and brand suffered major failure and embarrassment. Although it was my biggest challenge, it was the time that I re-discovered who I was and gained the strength to soar like the eagle I am.

Where do you find your POWER?

My "POWER" comes from my faith in God first. I also rely on my life lessons and the countless women whose lives I have impacted as the strength I need to keep building when I get tired. I constantly read the testimonials that have been sent to me as a reminder that I am on the right path and living in my divine purpose.

A PURPOSE-FULL LIFE

Author: Dr. Sherrie Walton

(Excerpts from the book, "Help, I'm Pregnant with Purpose")

The phone buzzed on the dining room table and "Mom" popped up on the screen.

'Hey Mom, how are you?' I asked.

With sadness in her voice she responded, 'Motherdear, went home to be with the Lord.' My heart immediately sank as I stared blankly while everything around me suddenly became a blur. Have you ever felt as if your entire world was spinning out of control? Have you ever felt as if something that you had meticulously organized and carefully planned, in a moment's notice took a deep dive? That explains how I felt the day I received the unexpected call from my mother.

'Okay, I'll call you back. Please keep me updated on the funeral arrangements,' and with that we hung up the phone.

I sat there for a little bit and began to reminisce on how both of my parents were burying both of their mothers just a few months apart. I also remembered my husband's words as he encouraged me just a month prior to say goodbye to my grandmother as we were visiting my parents, because he just felt she wasn't going to make it. I am so happy I listened. But even saying goodbye to her that final time did not prepare me for the reality that she had passed away.

Dealing with her death, as her self-proclaimed favorite grandchild was just one of the things that tugged at me during May of 2016. Two years before her death, I made a commitment to God that I would walk fully into the call on my life. I made a vow that I would stop running from ministry and helping others, the way I knew I needed to. I made a verbal agreement that I would go – even if I had to go alone. I was afraid but I was also tired of trying to figure things out on my own – tired of running. Do you know that feeling of submission due to exhaustion? It's a combination of emptiness, hopelessness, frustration and confusion, all bundled into one. If you know anything about Jonah, then you can probably visualize what it's like to run when you have a mandate on your life. I ran…and I ran…and I ran until finally there was no other choice but to throw my hands up and surrender. I would love to say that I willfully submitted – but that just wouldn't be the truth.

My come to Jesus moment sounded something like this, 'Well, God, I guess You aren't giving me a choice, so here I am.'

I often say that many people seem to have choices on whether they will submit. Me, on the other hand will witness every door shut in my face and every person I thought was necessary will leave in order to redirect me and force me in the right direction. (Yes, I know that He gives everyone a choice, so don't judge my relationship I have with Him.)

May 14, 2016 was the day when the "Mommy and Me Dream Bigger Tour" was heading to Dallas. I had been planning the conference for months and it was my first time ever hosting an event there. It was the second stop on the tour and so many things had transpired for me from the first event in January, including planning the event solo, making my own connections in a new city and doing it all without any major sponsorships or backing. I am thankful there were some dedicated women who believed in me and my vision, and despite all the things that were going haywire, they stood by my side as I ventured into uncharted territory. My biggest supporter and anchor was my husband, Christopher, and although he was running everything behind the scenes, he was the rock that held me up during one of the most challenging times of my life. He saw the vulnerable Sherrie that often questioned if I was good enough as I discovered who I was in this new space. The speaking circuit was not the most welcoming, as I often encountered women who expressed that my resume wasn't impressive enough to hold a room let alone host a conference. Thankfully, they were not the ones that called or anointed me. My support team reassured me that despite what it looked like, I would come out on top, I desperately hoped they were right.

When my mother called to discuss the funeral plans, she informed me that Motherdear's funeral would be held on May 14, 2016, the same day as my Mommy and Me conference. The funeral would take place in Miami while I was scheduled to be in Dallas.

Okay God...we have a problem. Do you want me to cancel the event and attend the funeral? I can't do both.

So many conflicting thoughts raced through my mind so I retreated to my prayer closet to pray. My closet has been my safe place for years, and words of comfort, direction and healing were so needed at that time. God speaks to me there. That day in the closet was dreadful. I am in no way comparing myself to Jesus Christ, but I received a little glimpse into what the garden of Gethsemane felt like. I put on my headphones and listened to Oceans by Hillsong and sat there with my legs crossed as tears rolled down my face while the song played.

'God, what are you saying to me?' I asked as more tears rolled down my eyes. In my spirit, I heard these words,

'You are in the middle of giving birth, and you must push. There will always be a reason for you to stop and turn back, but if you stop now, you will abort your purpose.'

Wait! What's happening? There were things that I understood about what was going on, but there were also many things that were a blur. Up until that time, I hadn't fully experienced the pain of birthing purpose. I was familiar with making bold moves; less than one year before that day my family relocated to Houston leaving everything and everyone familiar behind. Years before that I left my cushiony job in Corporate America to pursue my business fulltime. But as bold as those moves were, this pain felt different. Those were labor pains, this was the actual birthing process.

Why was I being faced with what seemed like one of the hardest decisions of my life, after I had surrendered all I had? Was I being punished? I had no doubt that missing this funeral would label me as disloyal, undependable, and break my trust with my family – something I valued more than anything. The direction I received went against what my heart was telling me to do.

Would God put something so difficult on my shoulders that would challenge everything I knew about loyalty and family? I questioned. *Would He tell me to choose the opposite path of what I felt was the right thing to do?* I had so many questions.

Those questions didn't change the reality that I had a decision to make, and I had less than two weeks to do it. I told my husband what I had heard in my spirit, and he held me tightly as I cried in his chest. He knew what I was up against. I decided to proceed with planning the event. I decided to step out on water. Now this is the part of the story where everything perfectly comes together and the heavens open while the dove ascends. *Well…not really!*

Actually, it was the total opposite. Just as I made the decision to proceed with the event, even more storms began to arise. The tickets did not sell as I thought they would. The sponsorship dollars that were promised were reduced last minute which affected me meeting the budget I needed. Houston, we have a problem. *Surely, I must be doing something wrong,* I thought. So I did what any believer hoping and wishing would do. I called a fast and prayed with my team as I called down the heavens. If I had to do a rain dance, I probably would have done that too.

'Keep walking, Sherrie!'

When the day finally arrived, I watched God move me out of the way as I submitted the event to Him. I stood in front of the attendees and told them that my grandmother was being celebrated in her homegoing service, but I was not there. Instead, I chose to be obedient to my assignment. That day I witnessed women's lives changed and the testimonies that emerged gave me the boost I needed to understand my sacrifice was not in vain. I gave birth to purpose and helped impact the lives of women. I won't be dishonest and say the process was easy. It didn't feel good to me then, but when I saw the results, I understood the why.

I share that very personal story with you because often times we admire people standing on stages around the world and we celebrate their results, but rarely do we know their process and their pain. I want to prepare you for the process and pain of giving birth to purpose. The process is the reason why many people stop halfway through and retreat. They lose sight of the promise and they focus only on the pain. I learned some unbelievably valuable lessons about purpose after my event. I learned,

> ➢ Your purpose is your light. It is the pre-destination of your life designed to bring help, healing, and clarity to others.

> ➢ Life does not miraculously fall in place because we make a decision to pursue our purpose.

- The hardest decision you will make will be to pursue your purpose.

- The bigger the impact, the bigger the obstacles you will encounter.

- Birthing purpose will be a spirit led act and there is nothing you can do relying on your human strength alone.

- The process is painful; however, the end results are worth it.

What Is Purpose?

Purpose is the reason for which something is done or created, or for which something exists. Purpose realized is the ability to use your inner gifts, personality strengths, wisdom and insight to impact and inspire the lives of others in a positive and productive way. Purpose is impactful… Purpose is unselfish… Purpose is your life's blueprint… Purpose is your "why".

Purpose is a seed. The birthing of your purpose is the producing of your seed. The harvest of your purpose is the legacy that you leave on the Earth, the testament that you lived. I define purpose as your life's work.

My passion is to help women discover and walk boldly in their purpose. In fact, most women I meet I encourage them to find out who they are outside of the roles and titles they wear. I challenge my married friends to re-discover those inner dreams they dreamt before they became a wife. I push those moms to remember the goals they had before their life became immersed with motherhood. As women it's easy for us to lose ourselves in our titles and neglect the inner girl inside of us longing to find her place in the world. This is a disservice not only to you, but it is a disservice to your Creator.

When I understood and accepted my purpose, women from all over the world started to connect with me. They were mostly professional women who had successfully climbed the corporate ladder and proudly displayed the word "Boss" on their chests. On the outside these women were the epitome of style and grace. Their hair was in place, their nails neatly manicured and their wardrobe looked as if they had stepped out of a Vogue magazine.

To the naked eye they looked like they had it all together. They were amazing, powerful and strong. Anyone looking at them would have wanted to be in their shoes. They had achieved great careers, money in the bank, and oftentimes a man on their arms. They said and did all the right things in public, posting motivational quotes, quoting scriptures and serving their community. They had multiple degrees and social proof to show they were on top of the world. But even with everything seemingly going well for them, something was missing.

Like clockwork, when I questioned whether they were living their purpose they would admit they weren't. It's not because they didn't want to. It is not because they lacked confidence. And many times surprisingly, it wasn't fear that was keeping them stuck. It was the busyness of life that kept them from sitting still long enough to hear direction from God. They would go on and on about how they were too busy to look after themselves; their career was demanding, and their children's lives consumed theirs. With so many extra-curricular activities, homework, and preparing dinner, there was hardly anytime left for them to think about themselves. If they were married or in a serious relationship, involved in their church or working a side hustle, the lack of free time was even more scarce. I became exhausted just listening to how hectic their schedules were – it changed frequently, sometimes hourly. The demands on them left little time for alone time. It was not their fault but somehow, they became caught up in the cycle. This is a familiar story of people who are busy in life but not fulfilling their purpose.

God does not speak in chaos; He speaks in the stillness of life.

Awakening of Purpose

I believe that discovering and walking in your purpose is just as important as breathing. Your purpose is the very existence of who you are, the reason that you have been put on Earth. Fulfilling your purpose gives your life meaning and motivates you to grow, give, evolve and become an unstoppable force. The opposite of this is aimlessly moving about just trying to find your way. That aimlessness appears in many forms. It is working a job you hate. It is being in a relationship that drains you and no longer serves who you are. It is picking a career because it seems to be the only option available to you. It is hoping and wishing that you happen to bump into happiness; dressed in a suit and neatly groomed. Living your life like this will bring you unfulfillment and a lifetime of restlessness. But I am sure you know this already, that is why you are here.

As you read this book I pray you start to feel an awakening taking place in your spirit. Maybe you have felt this way for some time now. The awakening may show up in one of many forms. For example, you start dreaming and believing you want more out of your life. You spend countless hours researching your special interest on the internet and reading books about it. You keep running into strangers that ask you if you are in a particular profession. You notice a recurring problem in others and before you know it you're telling them how to solve it. All of these scenarios are clues that God is sending your way to get your attention and cause you to question yourself and where you are right now. These are the clues that help you to discover your purpose. These soul-searching moments are the environments for the incubation and birthing of purpose. The more you start to inquire, the more you will discover that the answers are inside of you. The answers are in God's words. The answers are in others who have been assigned to you to help you birth your purpose. It is this shift that has drawn you to this book. You have dreams that you want to see fulfilled and you know that it is your birthright to have the promises manifested in this lifetime. You have been feeling uncomfortable and uneasy with your life and some of your life choices. The more uneasy you feel, the more frustrated you become.

You also know that who you want to be will require you to level up. You will have to get rid of the old thoughts, habits and undisciplined ways. You will have to release some relationships and say good-bye to some friends and family. Yes, something is happening. I call it the "Awakening of Purpose." It is the feeling you have not quite been able to identify but it's caused you to question if there is more to your life. It's the tingling you feel when you listen to people talk from the mainstage and pump you with motivational rants and chants that fire you up and cause you to wonder… What if? What if you went for it? What if you stepped out on faith? What if you stopped making excuses and tapped into your potential…? What if?

One of my favorite sayings throughout my life has been, 'When the teacher is ready, the student will appear.' One day Holy Spirit corrected me and said,

"When you seek, you will find, when you knock, the door will be opened to you" Matthew 7:7.

The next verse goes on to say, for all who seek will find. This means as long as you keep looking for your purpose you will discover it.

As a true believer in transparency I must tell you that purpose typically does not show up in your life only because you want it to, or because you expect it. In fact, it will probably show up in the most inopportune time when you least expect it. I shared my story with you about missing my grandmother's funeral earlier to let you know how difficult it can be to walk the unbeaten path, but also to show you there is victory on the other side.

Purpose, like a baby in your womb does not just go away. It grows inside of you until your body is ready to push. Just like in a natural pregnancy, there is a preparation that must take place before you give birth. I am ready to help you give birth. You are right where you need to be.

As you prepare to discover your purpose, I want you to acknowledge how amazing and significant you are to your Heavenly Father. It will be difficult for you to accept your purpose until you first learn to accept that you being here is not an accident. Life has a way of pushing us around and if we're not careful, we can become jaded and cynical and see ourselves as less than qualified for our assignment. You are chosen and qualified to fulfill your purpose. In fact, God chose you before the foundation of the world, and no matter what you have experienced up until this point, it does not change the fact that you are chosen.

Your life is not an accident. Despite how you arrived or the vessel used to birth you. Everything about you was purposely orchestrated and fashioned for you. The significance of the day you were born not only changed history but it signified a miracle performed in the earth realm. It doesn't matter if your beginning included a special fanfare by your parents, grandparents and loved ones, or if it entailed the silent embarrassment of a teenage mother giving birth in a cold lonely hospital room…it doesn't matter. It was special to God nonetheless. When you accept this truth and walk boldly and unapologetically in it, you will remove the pressure to receive validation from others.

God intricately and specifically formed you and put you together while you were in your mother's womb. Before she even knew you were there, He was behind the scenes creating you to be just the way you are. If you know anything about Him, you know that He doesn't do anything by accident and He surely doesn't do anything just because. You also know when He makes something He looks back and says that it is good. When He made you… He created a good thing.

Please allow me to stay here for a bit with you because I do not think we spend enough time celebrating ourselves. As women, we often spend so much time making a (happy) fuss over everyone else and we downplay ourselves to the point that many of us do not even celebrate our own birthdays. Many times we are stuck in the recurring cycles that scream to us; you're not enough or you don't matter...all lies!

God Can Use a Broken Vessel

I struggled for a long time thinking I was not worthy enough to fulfill my purpose to impact women around the world. I pushed the envelope far too many times and by the grace of God, and only because of his mercy, I was able to be delivered and set free from myself. I hurt people in the process and shattered the trust of some who trusted me, often those closest to me were the most affected. There were character flaws that needed to be dealt with. There were areas I needed to mature in. And there were bridges I had to amend. He allowed me to deal with most of these behind the scenes. Like any good father He allowed me the time to process the areas in my life that were broken and needed healing.

We live in a world where the judgment of others can limit us from fulfilling our purpose. We often think, what will they say? Will I come off as a hypocrite? I struggled with this as well. It's the reason I was too embarrassed to walk in my purpose. Allow my testimony to help you where you are. Maybe you aren't as messed up as I was, or maybe you are! No matter what, your purpose is still waiting for you.

I have been deep diving into the subject of purpose for over five years. During this time my views have matured as more revelation has been revealed to me through scripture. In my opinion, the subject of purpose is a topic that is ever evolving. Although the core applications of pursuing your purpose will remain the same, as well as the mindset and willingness required to step out on faith – the process of how you will activate and walk in your pursuit of purpose will look different from what you see others do. There is not a one size fits all for purpose.

I have concluded that we, as a society have been misinformed about pursuing purpose. If you ingest the commentaries that are floating around about the topic you'll probably feel inadequate or late to the party. You will feel that if you aren't making a profit with your purpose, you're doing something wrong. You will feel that if you aren't sitting with a million dollars in your bank account, there must be something wrong with you. You will feel that if you do not have the life others say you should – then maybe you've missed it. Allow me to debunk those lies.

Step into Discovery

When you are ready to walk in purpose, your first stop is discovery. Discovery is the first phase of identifying your purpose; this is your realization of self. In order to pursue purpose, you must first do the inner work to learn everything about yourself, your patterns, your quirks, your beliefs, your systems and your triggers. Your purpose has been showing up in bite-sized portions throughout your life, like clues to a riddle.

When you begin your discovery process, you will need to answer the following question.

- Who am I really?
- How old was I when I stopped seeing myself as fearfully and wonderfully made?
- What were the circumstances surrounding my shift in my perspective of myself?
- What are the gifts and talents that I have?
- How can I use these gifts to serve others?

To identify a tree, you must know what is planted in the ground. Seeds grow and bear fruit. Whatever is planted inside of you will grow. Now a tree is not permanent, you can always chop it down and pull up the roots. During your discovery you must be willing to uproot and destroy any idea that has formed because of a negative and toxic situation that occurred in your life, no matter how insignificant it may have seemed at the time.

During my discovery process, I had to revisit those earlier years of my life. I had to admit that feelings of insecurity and low self-esteem were planted at the roots of my tree. I was married with kids before I finally revisited those memories. My actions in business, my inconsistency in life, my fear of commitment, were all stemmed in those toxic thoughts I had about myself. My purpose could not be revealed until I was willing to accept, release, and forgive.

The enemy's assignment is to convince you that it is too late or that you've missed out on your purpose. He wants you to believe you have missed the train and that it will never come back around for you. He wants you to think that because you were a teenage mother, you endured a divorce, you experienced a physically abusive relationship, you flunked out of college or you filed for bankruptcy – that God can't use you or it's too late for you. This is simply not true!

Sadly, many of us had our purpose stifled in its infancy stages because we have existed in environments where people did not understand that our uniqueness was a blessing and not a curse. Part of the reason many people do not know their purpose is because they have been told over and over that who they are – their characteristic traits are not fitting. They are often criticized that they are too much of something and not enough of another, and they spend their lives searching for where they fit in. They waste so much of their time trying to fit in a box someone else made for them.

If you are still lost in discovering your purpose, do not worry you are not alone. Your purpose has been showing up in your life and because you are so familiar with yourself, you most likely overlooked the things that make you great.

Your purpose will require you to take an assessment of where you are today and what you envision for your future. Ask yourself:

- Do I feel fulfilled with my life today?

- Is what I am doing today leading me to the path of purpose?

- Have I been limiting myself due to my fears and insecurities?

- I know that I am great at (think about the thing that people are always calling on you to do)._____

- I am passionate about bringing hope, healing and restoration to _____ because_____

- What are some things I can do to bring betterment to this world? _____

There are certain characteristics that fashioned you into the woman you are today.

The purpose of life is not just to be happy. It is to be useful, to be honorable, to be compassionate. At the end is to have it make some difference that you have lived and lived well.

It's no doubt in my mind that greatness lives on the inside of you. I want to challenge you to take a deeper look at yourself and evaluate your life and your relationships.

There is a supernatural preparation that takes place before you birth purpose. When I was carrying my purpose, I could tell I was changing. I started to get a twinkle in my eye and a pep in my step. I couldn't think about anything else but starting my new project. I no longer wanted to waste time with people that weren't having any success in life. I no longer desired to gossip about people and what they were doing and who they were doing it with. I no longer wanted to just talk about changing but I really desired to become a better me in every area. I was willing to do the work to become a better me. I felt alive again. That empty feeling of why and I am on Earth and what's the purpose for my life started to subside. I felt my second life wind come back!

Being pregnant with purpose is a beautiful experience. Enjoy every moment of your growth and do not rush the process. During this time prepare yourself for the take-off. Prepare your environment as a mother preparing a room for her baby. Make any adjustments, get rid of the things that no longer serve you. Everything about you is changing – do not fight it.

Get around others that are fulfilling their purpose. You will easily recognize them. They will be the ones asking questions, being accountable and taking responsibility for their life and their decisions. When you meet them, they will have a glow and a passion for life.

How Will I Know?

The million-dollar question is often, "How will I know when I've found purpose?" There are characteristics to a purpose-full life, I have listed some below.

^ Inner Fulfillment

^ No shame

^ Growth

^ Inspiration to help others

^ No tolerance for certain people and places

^ Little to no procrastination

^ Goal driven life

^ No drama zone

^ Testimonials from others

If you can't check off at least half of the list above, I want you to challenge yourself to level up and discover purpose. For those of you who have discovered purpose, congratulations, now it's time for you to take someone else by the hand and help them give birth to their assignment. Our purpose is more than what affects our own little world. It's about serving others.

'I will live my life in such a way that I won't need a tombstone. My legacy will speak for itself.'

Dr. Sherrie Walton

Kineta Lewis-Harrison

What are the three words that best describe you?

Determined, Caring and Motivating.

What is the biggest challenge you've ever faced in life?

My greatest challenge was overcoming obstacles as a young single mother, moving to a new state and navigating life away from my family. I entered a place of uncertainty without financial security. I found myself at a fork in the road and chose the more difficult path that led to living a full life.

Where do you find your P.O.W.E.R.?

Staying connected to the eternal source of power sustains me. I listen to motivational videos daily, audio books and music that feeds my soul. The wisdom gained from a personal developmental coach keeps me plugged in and ready. The power of having a mentor guides me through difficult seasons. Celebrating winning moments energizes and empowers me to go after it. Learning from my mistakes gives me the power to not make that same mistake again. Lastly, utilizing the power of quiet time and rest that prepares me for what's to come.

Breaking Free from Your Comfort Zone to Live Your Best Life

Author: Kineta Lewis-Harrison

For I know the plans I have for you, says the Lord. They are plans of good and not disaster, to give you a future and a hope.

Jeremiah 29:11 (NLT)

Every morning we rise from our slumber to begin the day that awaits, breathing in life, entering the space we have created through our choices. As a wife, mother of three boys and manager of a premiere funeral home with demands in every area, the comfort zone could have been an attractive place to reside. Once comfortability was found, I struggled with the idea of being stretched. In our comfort zone we feel secure and in control. Our ever-changing lives require us to embrace the unknown.

At some point in the journey we enter a space of familiarity – the same people, processes and places. Some will say that this is normal. They are content doing the same thing every day. There are others who believe in order for them to live their best life, change must occur. Look around and consider, "Where have I been and what have I done in this place of comfort?" If we are not careful, as women, we can enter the comfort zone without knowing and remain there too long. Admittedly, life can become comfortable and stagnant. Unfortunately, there are many who get in this zone and never make it out. If we are not careful we can allow ourselves to become accustomed to living a particular life and before we realize it, opportunities for growth have passed by us, as time cannot be measured.

I believe comfort is one of the biggest enemies to us living a life beyond our wildest imagination. Did you know a change in your environment can open your eyes to things you've never seen before? Once your perspective changes, circumstances follow. I know first-hand what it means to dive into unfamiliar territory and receive the benefits of breaking free from my comfort zone. I am here to share personal and professional experiences with the expectation that it will inspire you to seek purposeful living and stretch yourself beyond comfort zones. As we share this time together, take an introspection and ask yourself, "Am I unproductively comfortable in this stage of the journey? Could I be living in a box that is limiting my potential to grow?" Let's dive into how my story unfolded.

Meeting Destiny

I encountered my destiny as a precarious six-year-old girl, running down the hall of my family's funeral home into a cold room filled with chemicals, aromas and people. I can still hear the mortician exuberantly shouting, "Get out! What are you doing here?" Grabbing the edge of the table to peek above my limiting view, I watched him work as he prepared someone for their final viewing. Instantly, I was intrigued. I am sure this scene may seem strange for some, I'll admit it's not a typical view for a six-year-old, but there was something remarkable about it. Purpose awakened in me that day.

There are moments in my life that stand out like golden nuggets that have now become treasures. One such moment is etched in my memory as it revealed what I would one day become.

Living an unpretentious life in Louisiana, I often spent time with my grandparents with little to do. My grandfather never let me forget the moment that confirmed I was called to be a funeral director. He quietly observed my actions. Every second of the old chime clock could be heard. The sound was a reminder that the beat of life ticked away, as our time is limited here. He sat reading the newspaper while I dressed my doll in a beautiful gown. She was covered with a towel and placed in a shoe box. My pink Barbie car led the way of our first procession to the baby doll cemetery. Cheerfully, the words resonated throughout the room, "I am having a funeral!" He smiled with pride, knowing I was born to do this. He shared this story with me throughout my journey. During difficult times it encouraged and reminded me that I was destined to be in the funeral business.

I also had a love for reading as a child. It stretched my thinking beyond the walls surrounding me. One example, *Ebony Magazine*, featured impactful African-American leaders in every issue. It highlighted those who accomplished great things in their community and they resembled me. When you see someone who achieves greatness against all odds, it gives you hope that one day success is attainable. This was another moment that planted the seed of progressive thinking. I perceived that those who achieved greatness had to live out of their comfort zone to make history.

Finding my destiny at an early age did not prevent experiencing uncertainty. It would have been ideal if everything fell into place and all of my dreams came true just as I had envisioned them, but that was not my reality. Life inserted obstacles; like my parent's divorce, a baby before the age of 19, and the death of a cousin that obstructed my view.

Adapting to Change

Life is filled with uncertainty. My parent's separation changed my perception on life expectations. They were the picture-perfect couple, both Southern University graduates with high ambitions. The radiant beauty of my mother reflected from the inside out. Her firm love was mixed with care and attention. An educator, who faithfully served in the church and introduced us to our Savior. My father was a strong man, a hard-working electrical engineer who loved God and his family. He believed in education and that a book could take us anywhere our minds imagined. My competitive nature was a gift from him.

The first hurdle I remember experiencing was understanding divorce. Learning to adapt to this was a devastating experience. The unexpected is inevitable and forces us to deal with things beyond our control. Thankfully, my step-dad entered my life during the crucial pre-teen period, when I needed him most. The unwavering support and structure provided me a solid platform for future ascension. They supported and instilled a quality of life that built my self-esteem. Daily affirmations were quoted in our home by my mother. Every morning I would awaken to his voice instead of the alarm clock. He became more than just a father figure, he was my accountability partner.

Asserting authority over my sisters was comfortable for me. Assuming I was in charge, I practiced being in "boss-mode" with them. They simply put me back in my place. My mother would remind me that my direct, expressive and out-spoken personality would be used in leadership one day. Little did she know, her words were accurate. Speaking positive words to me had a lasting impact over my life. Daily affirmations continue to be an important practice and are powerful in lifting my spirits when down, dispelling the fear that is sure to arise in uncertainty.

As life progressed, my choices led me into situations that complicated the process. I became a single mother after high school. While my peers were heading to their choice colleges, I was learning how to change diapers. My relationship with my son's father existed throughout high school. It became strained after he had to leave college and work to care for his son. I realized very quickly that it was going to be more difficult to reach my goals, but I was determined not to give up.

The following semester, I enrolled at Northwestern State University and worked a full-time job caring for disabled adults. Being a full-time mother, student and trying to fit in a social life was challenging. The downside was, I didn't get to experience "college life". This phase reminds me of my sister saying, "We make plans and God laughs". I thought I had life figured out, going through the motions, with ambitions unfulfilled. There was hope that his father and I would be able to push through our pains, however our relationship ended. We agreed as young adults to not let anything stand in the way of providing a fruitful life for our son and excelled in co-parenting. Although my plans had not worked out as expected, I learned to find the good in what seemed like the greatest disappointments. The discomfort of this season pushed me to find and better understand my purpose. Taking action restored my faith to believe that small steps develop into strides and lead to a greater purpose.

Finding Purpose

"The greatest tragedy in life is not death, but a life without a purpose. God's purpose is more important than our plans." Dr. Myles Munroe

We are called to fulfill a purpose; finding it is possible. It's never too late to figure out your purpose. Once you identify your calling, it aligns you with the fulfillment of your work. Purpose is like your fingerprint, uniquely special and only for you. It is the driving factor inside of you that came from the Creator who manufactured you in the beginning of time.

Entering into the death care industry at an early age revealed the pain and privilege of serving others, but it also introduced me to my purpose. I helped my family at the funeral home, absorbing every experience I encountered. Then, the unthinkable happened. My 22-

year-old cousin passed unexpectedly. I assisted with other family members before, but this was different. We were close in age. I was able to help restore my cousin so our family could have a fitting farewell. His mother expressed how peacefully handsome he appeared. It was one of the most difficult things to endure, but I knew this was not optional.

This experience taught me that tragedy takes you out of your comfort zone, however, it develops your inner strength. It pushed me to seek the best mortuary college and start the next phase of my journey. I realized this was a natural gift to be shared with those in need. After receiving my acceptance letter a few months later, I found myself at a fork in the road. Accepting the offer would require me to uproot from everything familiar and move to Houston, Texas. After considering the possibilities and reviewing the past, it was clear what I needed to do. Unfortunately, the person I was in a relationship with was not supportive of this change. The move would separate us.

Considering the reality that leaving your comfort zone can possibly en'd relationships is troubling, especially if you are dependent on them. This is the time when those who have traveled the journey with you need to be evaluated. If they are not meeting the expectations for your life to be successful and are weighing down your progress, consider making a change. Those preventing you from reaching your destiny must go! The decision to end a non-productive relationship freed me to run the race at my own pace, which was light years ahead of those behind. Time proved it was the best decision, even though it was uncomfortable. I chose to surround myself with people who empowered me to become better, removing those who caused stumbling blocks and prevented my growth. My future was waiting on me to make a move and I'm glad I did!

Growing up in Louisiana had many benefits, the close connections to family and friends created bonds that have lasted a lifetime. It was extremely difficult deciding to leave the place I called home. After many failed attempts to do things my way, I surrendered and trusted the divine plan. The conversation was short and direct when it was revealed to my parents that I was leaving. While they supported me, it was difficult to see me and their grandson move to another state. To help ease the pain of our separation, we stayed overnight.

The following morning, we were heading home. My mom stood in the driveway to see us off, as she often would. My son enthusiastically jumped into his car seat, while waving goodbye. Anxious for the next destination, I rushed to the driver's side. My mom abruptly stopped me and insisted I make sure my son was strapped in properly. I resisted initially, thinking to myself, the apartment was only a few minutes away. But like a good mother, she persisted, despite my opposition. Being obedient, I paused to check his straps and tightly secured them. With a smile, she exclaimed, 'Obedience is better than sacrifice.'

Within minutes of departing, while crossing the main roadway, we were struck on the passenger side by a speeding driver. The car bounced across the road like a Tonka toy and landed in the ditch. We walked away with minor injuries, but the hit was enough to total my car. Mom wasn't aware of the danger that awaited us, she simply used spiritual wisdom and authority to guide me. The short distance was no excuse for choosing a shortcut. I am thankful for the lesson learned that morning. Obedience is truly better than sacrifice and some shortcuts can lead to disaster, so avoid them at all cost.

"Obey God and leave the consequences to Him." ~ Dr. Charles Stanley

Transition

My momentum was stagnant after several unforeseen setbacks. When time came to execute the plan, resistance reared its head. Challenges often arise when living outside of your comfort zone. How you respond to challenges determines the outcome. For instance, I had to swallow my pride and ask for help, which was difficult for me. I confided in my godfather about my situation. I was reminded of the season he helped me overcome self-esteem issues, persuaded me to start carrying a purse and dressing professionally. I had a tomboyish attitude, not focused on my appearance. His influence inspired me to become the woman I am today. I altered my style before transitioning into an environment that would require business attire. He was always there for me, but this was on another level. I needed reliable transportation. He eagerly offered his car until I could get on my feet and didn't ask for anything in return. The invaluable support of those who believed in me was a driving force that catapulted me forward. Even though I felt overwhelmed, this act of kindness was a reminder of the little ways that God confirms His hand is guiding the situation. Jeremiah 32:27 – "I am the Lord, the God of all mankind. Is anything too hard for me?" (NIV)

I packed our belongings and we headed to Houston. Although it was a new and uncertain chapter in my life, I embraced it with optimism. Once settled, I went to the mortuary school for orientation. Total strangers stood at the entrance and welcomed me. My professors were the best and reaffirmed this was the right choice for me. Connections were made that simplified what I believed would have been a difficult process. When the move is right, there is a flow that is evident. Everything started falling into place. A friend I met while previously visiting the school helped me find a small apartment. He provided study notes and prepared me for what was to come. I was engulfed by the complexity of the curriculum, but did not let that deter me. When you determine in your heart that you can, you simply do it! I admit, the struggle was real, but it was worth it! I graduated mortuary school with honors, passed my boards and started my career.

"Nothing will work unless you do." ~ Maya Angelou

Upon receiving my license, I served as a funeral director and gained more experience at a local funeral home similar to locations in Louisiana. Although I had experience working in the business, this gave me the opportunity to adapt to working with people outside of family. The location had a large clientele and it challenged me. After several years of being stretched to the point of discomfort, dealing with the day to day monotony became familiar and uninteresting. I believe the urge for change occurs from outgrowing the capacity you are currently in, just like a shoe that no longer fits. I felt the discomfort of knowing there were more shoes that I needed to fill. I felt the squeeze of an environment that I had outgrown as there were no opportunities for me to advance.

After excelling in my career and experiencing great success, the door abruptly closed at that location. Sometimes a closed door will force you out of your realm of comfort to push you into your next level of success, even when you're not aware of it. Detours allow for time to recalculate. Instead of lamenting over what was, I rejoiced for what was to come. With the help of God and my older sister, I was able to maintain and refocus on strengthening my inner self. It was during this time of reflection that I connected with women of strong faith. They remained a source of hope and strength during my transition. Their shared wisdom inspired me to hang in there even during times of loneliness and doubt. Being in this place of discomfort was working for my good, but I could not see or feel it at the time. When I began to lose heart, a special lady encouraged me to remain faithful to God and He would remain faithful to me. That lady would one day be my mother-in-law, unbeknownst to me. Had I given up in that season, my husband may have missed meeting me. A few weeks later, the one who insisted on encouraging me, introduced me to my husband. We were inseparable from that point forward. We committed our lives to each other the following year and were married where we first met. This love story was truly written by God and continues after 14 years of marriage. "Looking unto Jesus the author and finisher of our faith." Hebrews 12:2

New Beginning

As months passed, my passion to be in a new environment led me on a pursuit to find a company that offered opportunities for advancement, security and longevity. My search ended at the second largest funeral home in Houston, which initially intimidated me because of its size. I never operated in a facility of that capacity. Thoughts of inadequacy entered my mind as I wondered if I would be a good fit for a large company or have the ability to perform at a location that was historically known for not being diverse. Those very thoughts brought me to the assumption that I would probably not qualify for a position, especially as a newly licensed director. My assumptions were surprisingly incorrect. I interviewed with an affiliate location a few months prior. The manager promised he would hold my resume after the initial impression of meeting me. I usually do not believe the hype from others, however, I was grateful that he kept his word and referred me to an affiliate location. I received a call a few weeks later and was offered a position to start immediately.

This was truly out of my comfort zone and required me to learn new cultures, service etiquettes and personalities that were undoubtedly different than my usual surroundings. By jumping into the pool when the water was troubled, I was able to ride the wave for over 15 years. Hard work and dedication to support the people around me led to several promotions and honorable recognitions. Just when I was comfortable in one role, they would transition me to another, never allowing me to be complacent, consistently challenging me to excel and set attainable goals.

I eventually became familiar in the place that was once new and confusing. I finally had financial growth and stability in my role. During a discussion with leadership, I was asked to take on a new assignment that would require me to travel, which I did not receive well at first. In addition to the growth in my career, I had excelled in my personal life as a wife and a mother of three boys. Frequent travel would complex not only my home and family life, but also the team that I managed. They would all have to learn to navigate and function in my absence. I was reassured by my family and leadership that they would support my decision. We strategized a plan to ensure that both environments continued to thrive while I was away.

Life forced me to choose the path of resistance again and learn something new that would eventually propel me into the next phase of the journey. Surprisingly, it was one of the best experiences in my career. I was able to learn new things, share the passion of my calling with colleagues and support the organization during the largest requisition in our company's history. Had I focused on the known cons of traveling, instead of the pros of the possibilities that it could bring, I would have aborted all of the joys I received by simply giving it a try. I kept an open mind about leaving my familiar environment. It takes courage to step out to explore unfamiliar paths. As a result, doors were opened to future assignments simply because I changed my zip code for six months.

"Be strong and courageous and do the work. Do not be afraid or discouraged, for the Lord God, my God is with you. He will not fail you or forsake you…" –1Chronicles. 28:20

Not long after returning from that assignment, promotion directed me to manage another historic and premiere location. The years of experience and faithfulness in my previous roles led to that opportunity. The surprise of going into a location with new people and old habits, allowed me to tap into reservoirs of my soul and soar to greater heights. The location achieved great success. The reward of seeing others win was gratifying and humbling. When your heart is focused on other's success, your success is guaranteed. The fulfillment of knowing those on your team are positioned for greatness is revealed when you see the final results. It brought me joy watching the team advance as a result of choosing to be uncomfortable. I helped others learn how to step into the unknown and trust the journey. Thereby, earning "location manager" of the year and exceeding quota goals.

When we step into the unknown, it not only benefits us, but it allows others who are connected to walk into their destiny. We had a continuous flow of knowledge that increased the capacity of those under my wings. The team was adequately trained, our goals were accomplished and reorganization of the department was complete. My previous location needed a general manager. I served well as senior/lead director and assistant manager there prior to being promoted. Because of the consistent flow of knowledge, my assistant was ready to walk into the open position. The leadership had full confidence in my abilities, however, because of the magnitude and responsibility of the role, disbelief set in. After escalating my concerns as far up the totem pole as possible. I questioned if I was ready to take on the task of managing where I spent most of my career.

This was a major responsibility, far more than I ever wanted. I knew how difficult it would be to maintain a healthy work environment in a place that had significant challenges. With all doubts present, I took the leap! By doing so, I became the first African-American woman within a century of the location's history to lead the entire establishment. One thing life has taught me – change is inevitable. Leaving your comfort zone is where success lies. Find a way to start moving today!

Poised to Leave Your Comfort Zone

I was a panelist at our company's first women's conference. I connected to like-minded successful women. The camaraderie inspired me to pour my life into women who desire to expand their territory, stretch beyond limiting borders and reach for the prize that awaits. In preparing to leave your comfort zone, think strongly about developing others. As we look forward to what is next, it may be dependent on the progression of others. In discovering my path, every promotion required me to lead people that were once peers. Once in my career, I managed a previous supervisor and was tasked with keeping the culture positive. It was uncomfortable leading someone that once led me, however, we functioned well together and reached several goals. It's hard to think about others when you are trying to get ahead, but it has proven to be beneficial in my journey. I was always taught to train my replacement so when the time of transition comes, we would be ready.

"*Lead Simply*" by Sam Parker is one of my favorite leadership resources. It explains how we should model the behavior we want to see in our team. I choose to lead by example, connecting with people by building relationships and creating trust. To teach others how to step out, we must model the behavior. When opportunities are available, encourage growth. Training your replacement ensures consistent development within the organization. Have confidence that your value and position requires forward thinking if you want to live out of the box. In spite of feeling irreplaceable, I have learned that transition eventually comes and we can be poised for change.

Involving others ensures that when you step out, someone else can step in. To lead by listening, showing, sharing, and inspiring, we expand our knowledge and that of our team. It empowers us to take on different challenges with surety that the space we leave can be filled. Having meaningful conversations about what is next and why each person's involvement is so important, opens the door of opportunity. There are many women needing encouragement, mentorship and advice as they travel in unfamiliar territory. We can learn and be their guide as we embark on new horizons.

Ready, Set, Go

Life has taught me it will never be easy to leave our comfort zone and live out of the box. It is a requirement as we evolve into our roles as leaders in society. Women are taking on leadership roles like never before and I want to challenge you to elevate your life to your next level. This can only be done by stepping out of your comfort zone. Don't be afraid to stand in your POWER. Boldness is required to seize the moment and live your best life. The Father knows what's best for you, seek Him for understanding. After submitting to His will for my life, I see His hand operating in every area. My hope is that you will be impacted by reading my story and take the leap. As we embrace life's surprises we can hold to the truth that never changes.

"Have I not commanded you? Be strong and courageous. Do not be afraid; do not be discouraged. For the Lord, your God is with you wherever you go." Joshua 1:9 NIV

When tempted to remain comfortable, think of the possibilities that await us, if we would choose to have the life we want to live. Being uncomfortable propelled me to dream and take the next steps. It led to defying the odds, overcoming fears and finding strength to endure. Keep pushing, do not quit, set SMART* goals and when you reach them, set more! Choose to be a woman that conveys value, inspires hearts, motivates minds and engages those who support your vision. In my profession, I am reminded daily that tomorrow is not promised; time waits for no one. Today, we have the ability to choose the life we want to live. Let this fact propel you to dream and think of the next steps you wish to take. There are risks involved with stepping out of your comfort zone. Don't allow fear of the unknown to stop you before you begin. Take the necessary steps: Accept the risk of leaving your comfort zone, adapt to change, enter a life of purpose, transition to the next phase and embrace new beginnings.

Break free from your comfort zone and live your best life, now!

SMART Goals

(Bogue, Robert. Use S.M.A.R.T. goals to launch management by objectives plan.")[1]:

Specific – target a specific area for improvement.
Measurable – quantify or at least suggest an indicator of progress.
Achievable – specific objectives can be reached.
Realistic – state what results can realistically be achieved, given available resources.
Time-related – specify when the result(s) can be achieved.

---

[1] Bogue, R. (2013). Use S.M.A.R.T. Goals to Launch Management by Objectives Plan. TechRepublic.
http://www.techrepublic.com/article/use-smart-goals-to-launch-management-by-objectives-plan/

Meet Araceli Avionn

What are three words that best describe you?

Motivated, Driven, Humble.

What is the biggest challenge you have ever faced in life?

The biggest challenge I have faced would be balancing the obstacles that came with being young, female, and African American in the workforce of leadership. I have been told many times that I had to walk lighter, talk softer, and be more flexible than others because I was an African American female. Learning to adjust to be respected without changing the compass of who I am and what I believe in has always been my focus.

Where do you find your P.O.W.E.R.?

I find my "POWER" through my drive to provide a positive example of excellence for my son. I aspire to be the proof that hard work and dedication can change the trajectory of one's life. Also, mentoring and developing others so that we win as a team is fulfilling. The ability to guide others in the direction of success while beating the statical odds stacked against me is a healthy reminder that my purpose is greater than words can explain.

Finding Your Invisible Strength

Author: Araceli Avionn

Invisible strength... Is there really such a thing? The Webster's dictionary defines invisible as "impossible or nearly impossible to see by the eye." It also defines strength to be, "the property of being physically or mentally strong."

In my 34 years of life I have seen the highs and lows of family, friends, coworkers, and acquaintances. I have provided a listening ear, my unsolicited advice, and even a shoulder to cry on. On October 2011, I began my personal storm before the calm. It is only now, almost a decade later, that I can speak on finding my invisible strength. Finding my peace amid adversity was not an easy road, however, through perseverance I made it to the end of the rainbow to see the sunshine following the storm. Invisible strength appears in your life when you are at your lowest moment, at the point of breakdown. It is at that point when your heart tells you to fight on, that you are not just living for yourself. Invisible strength allows you to brush yourself off and wipe away the tears. It is as if someone has physically picked you up and helped carry you with your burden. My path to becoming stronger within my invisible strength, took taking a moment to isolate myself from "what was happening to me" and deciding how I wanted to react to my current environment. It was a mindset that I had to change. Changing my mindset and making the determination that I would not allow myself to become, my situation was the first step to becoming a stronger version of myself. I isolated myself from my friends and family for a short period of time to become comfortable with the direction that my life had taken me in.

That is the moment when you decide that you will not be defeated. It is time to start a new journey, but with this journey comes acceptance, anger, hurt, denial, struggle, embarrassment, and ultimately forgiveness. This will lead you to finding your happiness.

So, the answer is yes. There is such thing as "invisible strength." I define this as the ability to become a stronger person from deep within mentally. To become a better you from the inside out, this is clearly impossible for anyone else to see. But if you allow yourself to grow, what is impossible for the naked eye, will become apparent to the open heart.

The back story...

On October 2011, I found out I was pregnant with my first child. In many eyes this would be a moment of excitement. For me it was more of a moment of confusion, fear, and disbelief. Although having a child had always been an ultimate "want" of mine, it was not the ideal time to bring a baby into the world. I was in the final year of graduate school, working full time and caught up in an on and off relationship with my ex-fiancé.

In 2009, my college boyfriend proposed me, and we planned to marry in 2010. Upon graduating with my undergraduate degree in December 2009, I was offered a full-time management position from a great company out of state. I accepted, relocated and awaited my fiancé to relocate with me. That did not happen, so I called off the wedding. I could not contemplate at the time, a long-distance engagement and a long-distance marriage. *How exactly does that work?* We remained friends and ultimately started dating again when I relocated back to Houston in 2011 after receiving a promotion.

Dating led to a more romantic relationship which lead to my pregnancy.

A month into the pregnancy and my son's father made the decision to abandon me and our unborn child and focus on his own life. There was much anger, hurt, and sadness that followed for me. I sulked around for a bit and had the typical female reaction of sending messages to him hoping he would change his mind. Eventually, the mental and emotional abuse became too much to handle. This is not what I had imagined pregnancy to be like. I realized that the unhealthy relationship with my son's father, which escalated from the best of friends to toxicity, caused more anxiety and stress to an already high stress situation.

The breakup led to the start of an exceptionally long nine-months of pregnancy. My plate consisted of working fulltime combined with the pressure of having eight months left to complete my graduate degree program. I had to make the decision on what to prioritize and what to not dwell on. I didn't want to become a statistic; becoming pregnant and dropping out of graduate school. It had always been my goal to obtain my graduate degree and I was on track to be the first in my family to complete such a major accomplishment.

It was after a long night of working on an assignment that I made the promise to myself that I would not give in to what society stated was the "right way" to live your life. Society led me to believe I should finish school, get married, build a future with a significant other, then have children and magically I would live happily ever after. I now laugh at statistical views. It was that night that I found my invisible strength. I created an achievable plan – if I stayed focus. The plan consisted of continuing my full-time job, completing graduate school on time, mending challenged relationships with family, and preparing to become a mother all in the seven months I had left prior to the arrival of my son.

Not becoming a statistic

Growing up I always knew I wanted and expected more for myself than what I was exposed to. Being raised in 3rd Ward Houston Texas, which was historically known for being the inner city more urban lower class "ghetto" side of the town. I can remember my parents not allowing me to go across the street to a best friend's house because they felt it was too dangerous to be in others' homes and being on the street with the "rift raft" as they would call it. Of course, we would find our way over there in the day and back home prior to them returning from work; we have all pushed the limits when we were younger. There were no accolades growing up as I did, and the school district would not be my first choice for many raising children.

Growing up in the inner-city school district was proven to be tough at times, because I lived more of a sheltered life in terms of rules and freedom, at most of my schools attended I was labeled as "not black enough". As a pre-teen and teenager, it was tough trying to find my way and "become blacker" in the sense of culture. What does that even mean? Well for me, it meant changing my outfits, my dialect, my attitude, basically molding myself into the image of the perception of others' expectations. It became so easy to lose myself. I was the teen that would try to outsmart the adult. I had an attitude and reacted quickly to intense situations because I thought this would allow me to fit in and not be pushed around. Teenage girls were mean in high school. I had my fair share of challenges with maintaining being a high school athlete who loved the status of being in the "in crowd". The good news was that I did make it through high school and graduated in the top 5% of my class while being class president 3.5 years of my time there.

As I grew and continued to find myself, I knew I did not want to continue this way of living in my adult life. In terms of continuing to mold myself into the person others expected. I also came to realize there were more women and men who shared similar stories. This has also been a driving factor in becoming a mentor to others. I did not have anyone to guide me through the difficult moments of being a teenager past my high school track coach whom kept us at arm's length in terms of grades and disciplinary expectations to remain eligible for sport. My parents were tough on grades, straight "A's" were the expectation and the only way I could convince them to allow me to continue sports. However, past that we did not have an open dialogue. I have often felt the need to just "figure it out". This has rolled over into my parenting style as well. I am the first one to say I am terrible at taking unsolicited advice to the right and wrong way to raise a child. I was told having a child prior to getting married was backwards and the wrong way. To all those who expressed that, all I can say is, 'Look at me now!' We can do anything with determination and a plan.

The same drive and discipline I had as a child, definitely rolled over into my pregnancy, I was very hard on myself. I would not allow myself to complain because I chose the cards, I was dealt. I pushed myself as if I already had someone depending on me. I was the only one who could support my vision on the direction I wanted my life to go in. I took ownership of my life. I can remember the day I walked into my boss's office to reveal that I was pregnant. I asked him not to mention it to anyone because I did not want to be treated differently in what was already a male dominated field. I was fearful of losing my job because of the demand to which I supported within the workforce. I think I put in more hours after becoming pregnant just to prove it would not affect my contribution to the company. I ultimately worked five months before anyone knew I was pregnant and eventually point my growing stomach was finally noticeable.

My job was very physical in the sense of working in a distribution center that required you to walk across "catwalks" with gaps from the 2nd floor looking down to only nets, manage and oversee the unloading and loading of semitrailers, and audit shipments. I knew I had to work twice as hard when the vice president (a male) explained to me while I was six months pregnant, that he did not care that I was pregnant, that the expectations remained the same. So, I hopped across cat walks, helped load/unload trailers if my team fell behind and completed all my managerial reports daily without fail. I did not miss a beat. To this day I believe the vice president wanted me to fail as there were outlining racial challenges, I faced with him and adding a pregnancy to the mix made the situation more complicated. However, I would not give him the satisfaction of failure and I would not allow myself to give up.

I had a supportive direct leader during this period of my life. He taught me leadership skills to which I utilize to empower my teams to this day. I learned perseverance during this period in my life. I learned to never give up or give in to what others want of you, when it's a negative forum. Perseverance was so important to me during my pregnancy because I felt as if I was running a race, and it was not how fast I finished, it was the goal of finishing completely which was important.

Staying Focused on My Goal

In the back of my mind I knew I had a point to prove to myself and to others. So often society perceives women who are single and pregnant as a negative occurrence in one's life. I had already seen firsthand peers, and associates who encountered the same circumstances and allowed themselves to lose focus on their personal passion. However, the single most important thing that kept me focused during the pregnancy was knowing that I had another person who was depending on me now and for many years to come.

Because I was able to manage both my personal and career life, I understand the importance of setting goals and sticking with them. Staying on track is a job within itself. I would set small attainable goals which would help me reach each milestone. Setting attainable goals, allowed me to not become overwhelmed with the demands of life. With long-term goals which would take longer to accomplish, I was unable to see the light at the end of the tunnel, which means there were not many opportunities to celebrate myself. I celebrated the small wins to stay motivated and encouraged.

How to Attain Your Goals

Many people create goals for themselves but don't take the necessary steps to reach them. There are certain things you must implement to see your goals materialize. Visuals and accountability checks are crucial for your success. I created a timeline of action items to help me reach each milestone. Timelines are important because they provide a daily visual to hold you accountable. I created visible timelines to post where I could see each day, as well as a digital calendar to send me reminders. These are the two methods I implemented to ensure I earned my degree from graduate school and I was able to complete my courses for graduate school one month following the birth of my amazing son. As a matter of fact, I was in the hospital studying for finals to ensure I did not miss a beat. Can you imagine walking across the stage and having your child there to witness it? I can and have the photos to remind him in the future that nothing is impossible. This was a defining moment in my life and would set the tone for putting a drive behind my passions, I had become the first one in my family to earn a graduate degree. Now it was time to focus back on my career.

Key things to remember on how to prioritize the items that matter are:

- Most importantly – create a list of tasks.

- Identify your timelines for completion.

- Understand what's urgent and what can be completed later.

The Next Level

After I obtained my new degree, I knew I wanted to elevate in my career as well. During my leave from work, I began seeking new career opportunities outside of my normal scope of work. At that time, my area of expertise was logistics operations. While working within operations was my comfort zone, I knew I needed a variety of skillsets to ensure I was marketable. I interviewed for a human resource logistics role and landed it. I could not believe it; I was transitioning from operations to human resources. Only six weeks following the birth of my son, a new opportunity had presented itself and I was all over it!

While I write this story with excitement, I can remember the transition was not as easy as I had expected. I did not start off on the right foot, I missed my first day of work. How unbelievable is that? I had been traveling in the night before, had an emergency and had to call in to work. That was strike one on the first day. While this was embarrassing, I walked in to work the next day with my head held high ready to concur the position. The learning curve however was a tough one, I did not have the same confidence in this new position. It took me putting in extra hours at work when I could, taking home handbooks to learn policies and procedures, and relying on peers to help show me the way. Even with all the extra work I was putting in, things were tough, that was until I found my routine.

Create a Routine

I created a routine to help organize and regain my focus. Prior to developing a routine and finding my rhythm, I was all over the place; balancing the demand of being a new mom and a creating success in my career. I had a problem with asking for help, I wanted to do it all. I felt as if since it was my decision to have a child its solely my responsibility to ensure all the pieces fell correctly into place. I must admit I may still have that sentiment however I have learned to appreciate routines and asking for help when I am backed into a corner. My routine was something simple.

- ***Rest:*** I had to create realistic window to allow for rest.

- ***Asking for help:*** I had to ask for help in picking up my son so that I would not have the added stress of fighting two hours of traffic.

- ***Preparation:*** When it came to mealtime, I purchased prepared meals. It is the small things in life that we often overlook that can help simplify our lives.

Becoming an instant single parent was not an easy transition. And the referenced focus and routine has been instrumental in maintaining my day to day sanity. Speaking candidly, even with all the focus I have still made many sacrifices that affect my son's and my ability to have the extended quality time that I would prefer. I have lost friendship, not pursued relationships, and became engulfed in work because it is what provides for our family.

The need to be perfect and/or overcompensate because there is only one parent in the household has proven to have its ups and downs. My son will remind me every now and then that I cannot go to lunch on a weekly basis, allow him to be a "car rider" at school every day, ride his bike home with his friends, as he see from his classmates with the stay at home moms. It hurts my feelings at times, but I know that in the long run he will understand the sacrifices that we have made. At least I hope so because although I cannot make up to those smaller things, I have been able to travel the world with my son and expose him to more at the age of seven than many can see at the age of seventy.

Success is Mindset

Obtaining success in my life and career has been a mindset. Nothing has been given to me and luck has not gotten me far. While I do believe there is truth behind being blessed and favored, even that comes with the expectation of putting the "work" behind it. There have been a couple surprising moments in my career which have not been ideal and difficult to navigate through. I can remember an employer restructuring the company layout and providing severance packages. The package was enough to maybe pay the bills for two months. This came as a complete surprise. The level of stress to find a new job before being placed in a financial bind became the new goal and this goal was not easily obtained. While at the time I was also an adjunct professor, that would not pay all the bills. Applying for jobs became my new nine to five job. I remember submitting ten to twenty applications a day, and this went on for months. Submitting application with no response. Taking interviews for jobs which were misleading and ultimately did not accept. Having to decline low ball job offers because I was confident in my worth and would not accept being underpaid for my education and experience. What I hoped would take thirty to sixty days had now turned into five months.

This rigorous circle and time in my life led to many rough days of questioning; had I made the right decisions in life. I had to dig deep into my belief and practice what I preached in terms of finding my "invisible strength". Yes, I could allow myself a bad day, but I could not allow myself to stay there. 'Cry and get over,' this is what I would tell myself, 'man up Araceli.' And that is exactly what I did. This was one of the toughest times for me in my life, I didn't talk to anyone about this setback outside of my best friend and my sister. I think I may have told my sister because she had figured it out, she knew my routines and I rarely deviated from them. Any deviation for too long I am sure anyone could have figured it out.

During this time, I convinced myself that everything does happen for a reason and made the best of the extra time I had to spend with my son. I was able to do things like; pick him up early, hand out longer at parks, and not always feel as if I was in a rush. I allowed myself to get lost in the positivity of building a greater bond with my son, and trust that I would eventually find an employer who I felt would allow me to continue my growth in my career while providing the platform to lead and mentor through the position to which I would hold in the organization. In the long run, having the patience and faith paid off. I accepted a job with a great company that allowed me to grow, mentor and develop the leadership team underneath me.

This opportunity was another great way to continue my path of leadership development. Along with great new beginnings, it brought the continued obstacle which I have faced many times in my growing career; being the youngest leader amongst my peers. It has proven to be more difficult leading down and being taken seriously leading up. It can be challenging managing individuals from both sides of the spectrum. On one hand I would lead employees who were old enough to be my parent, and they were resistant to taking directions because from their point of view they had more experience in completing the task asked, and/or they were not open to any changes for implementation. On the other hand, I would lead employees who were very similar to age, so they were resistant, because from their point of view they did not want to be given a directive from someone their age and would blur the lines of leader verses peer. While wanting to remain consistently respectful to both groups, I learned to change my approach to reach my audience. I took being more relaxed and playful with the more mature teams and stern and to the point to the younger teams. Being flexible to adapt to my environment and being receptive of feedback is what has allowed me to obtain the "buy in" and trust of others.

Challenging myself professionally and personally has helped me to build the character to strive higher achievements. Never becoming complacent in life has taken me far. Wanting more for my son than I had, has pushed me farther. My drive for wanting him to be presented with opportunities to which I did not, has kept me focused. From better neighborhoods and education, to long term generational wealth, my goal is to set the foundation for a positive future. Finding that one thing that motivates you is an exceptional way to give you the extra boost when you are down. I always strive to continue to learn. I keep track of my progress for my small and large goals. I don't get lost in comparing myself to others. We do not all have the same journey.

How I Inspire Others…

I often look back on my life and become overwhelmed with how blessed I am, given the obstacles I have endured. An African-American female from 3rd Ward Houston, Texas, is now a part of a senior leadership team for a major leading industry company, obtained my undergrad and graduate degree, adjunct college professor, and upon conclusion of this writing, I will add published author to the list.

Wow, I am so inspired and grateful, it drives me to lead and inspire others. Throughout my life experiences I have learned that everything that I have successfully navigated through has provided me with the strength to support others. Being able to lead others through areas which I struggled with in the past provides me with a level of fulfillment I could not obtain simply by just living. Within my leadership career I joined many mentoring initiatives, which allowed me to guide the future leaders to reaching their full potential.

Mentoring college students has been a passion of mine for a long time. For me, college was a time of trying to find myself making the transition from high school to completely being independent a year later. I made the decision to move out of my parents' home at the age of 19. With this decision, I had to work two jobs while going to school full time just to get by. Wow, was that tough, however, I told myself 'once I move out then I cannot fail and return home. I did not have a mentor to help me navigate through my decisions with their past experiences and lessons learned, that may have been like mine. Mentoring and providing the "how" behind decisions I have made has provided others with options on personal goal balance.

Within my career, I have shared my story many times with employees who want to do more but have not because they are not aware of opportunities that are available. Opportunities which can flourish if they allow themselves to work a little hard and believe in themselves on a higher level. I strive to connect with the individuals who assume I may not be relatable because of the position I am in. I do not lead with my title or position at work. I find a way to be relatable to all my employees. Whether it is watching sports, a television show I would generally never watch, trying out a new restaurant, I'm willing to do it all so that I can engage with the team in morning meetings. Now I have employees who will visit me in my office to provide updates on personal and professional matters. Creating that safe zone where people can be themselves has been important to building the rapport that "I am here to help"

I am not ashamed or afraid to express where my life journey began and the path to which it has taken me. Many individuals from where I was raised do not make it to the level of leadership or life goals to which I have, often because the picture on the other side of the coin is not what is shown by society. Transparency builds trust within others. I have not "lost who I am" to conform to what society thinks is perfect and/or the right way of doing things. Inspiring is about showing others there are many paths to arriving at the finish line, and in many cases your timeline will not be the same as your neighbor's timeline. Work at a pace to achieve goals that works for you.

Striving for excellence will forever be a focus of mine. Over the past nine years I have made many decisions which have led me to become the woman, mother, leaders, and mentor that I am. I do not regret any of the decisions which I have made. However, I have made several decisions that have become lessons to learn from. We have all been there I am sure. Moving forward, I plan to continue the momentum of mentorship for the youth and adults who may find it difficult to navigate from the box society wants to place us in based on our background.

At the beginning of this chapter I took you back to 2011 where it all started. Fast forward nine years later, my son and I are living life to the fullest. We travel the world and we make great memories. It is finally getting easier with him slightly understanding why I need to work and why he does not live the same life as his friends in school.

Succeeding at parenting is my first priority. My hope for you after reading this chapter is that you can pinpoint an area of motivation to strive and develop from. Understanding that what we call failures are lessons and steppingstones to the next great thing. It may not be the most comfortable task but finding your invisible strength in the times of when you feel as though the odds are against you is the best time to start. This is when you regroup, show up and show out in areas you did not previously think you could excel at. Finding your invisible strength will take courage in challenging yourself to let go of old habits to build new patterns of structure and releasing unhealthy relationships to build new ones. This is all necessary to become a better version of yourself. I cannot express enough how becoming a stronger and more confident version of myself has allowed me the courage to take risk that I in the past would have "played it safe on". Life is about taking chances and when I finally believed in this concept, I began to live larger. Don't give up and believe in yourself when no one else will. Along with critiquing yourself which comes easy to most of us, you should always be your biggest fan! I'm rooting for you!

Meet Dr. Linda Bell-Robinson

What are the three words that best describe you?

Resilience, Determined, Forgiving.

What is the biggest challenge you've ever faced in life?

My biggest challenges in life is with health issues in my family. As a teenager I was diagnosed with Sarcoidosis, a condition in which rashes appear in the lungs, on the skin, or on the lymph nodes. The next was when my father was diagnosed with Leukemia-the news devastated us. Finally, today's health challenge is caring for my older brother who is a double stroke victim. I still believe we are overcomers.

Where do you find your P.O.W.E.R.?

I get my POWER from trusting and believing in God who has never once failed me. In addition, my strength comes from my upbringing. My parents always pushed us to be the best we could be. Not only did I receive POWER from my parents, but from my immediate and extended family as well. They are my boon companions and knowing that I have their support is more than enough to keep me encouraged. Finally, my POWER comes from my husband; he is the "wind beneath my wings" and he empowers me to stand boldly and unflinching in public places where my voice can be heard.

Chapter 4

Living Life on Your Own Terms

Author: Dr. Linda Bell-Robinson

I am at a crossroads, contemplating a new chapter in the "Dr. Linda Bell Robinson-Morgan's" book of life! It's exciting, it's scary, and it's humbling all at the same time. The opportunity to reflect on my journey, on my life, and to expose my humanity is mind-boggling to say the least! The beautiful part is that I'm open, but have no idea how the mission and the story will play out. At this moment, I find strength and courage in my thoughts, and I possess a clear vision, as well as remnants of beautiful dreams in my soul. I wait patiently, expecting and prepared for the blessings, the lessons, and the battles that I will face because that's life, and life requires GRIT. There is this small voice repeatedly telling me that there is more to do, more assignments to fulfill my destiny and purpose. There are bigger and better opportunities at the next intersection specifically designed just for me. Do you hear and listen to your voice? We all have an inner voice that directs and guides us, and it's up to us to listen or not. I love my inner voice. It has protected me in so many ways throughout my life.

On my Facebook page are the words, 'Living life on my own terms; that is what I do and enjoy every moment.' Now, don't get me wrong, I respect rules, and I live by what is deemed to be the right thing even when no one is looking. But, I have learned, and am still learning, not to allow anyone to speak over my life or to unwisely advise me on what God has for me. Before reading my story, I would like to offer these three thoughts as guiding points:

1. There will always be someone or something to challenge you in your decision as to where you want to go.

2. No obstacle can stop what God has for you.

3. Stop and think before making any permanent decisions over what may be a temporary problem.

Looking Back to Move Forward

As I move into a more mature season of my life, I wonder what might my eulogy be. Will people talk about how hard I worked? Will they share stories about my mindset to accomplish any goal that I set out to achieve? I have to laugh because the truth is I missed so many goals for not believing I could do it. However, my inner voice would not leave me alone. It was the voice of reason constantly telling me that I could do all things through Christ, and that I could achieve any and all things, with faith.

Thinking about my eulogy, I hope that people will say:

- She was underestimated but never gave up!

- She was kind and always offered words of inspiration!

- She was faithful and became empowered by empowering!

I did not know until later in my life that these traits of never giving up and of being kind and faithful are the best traits a person can have. I knew early in my life that I was blessed with the gift of giving and caring. I loved people, and for the most part, most people liked me. Notice, I said *"liked"*. Some people will dislike you for the red dress you wore, or because you walked past them and unintentionally, failed to speak. Early on, God blessed me not to worry about trivial things, and He taught me never to worry about things that are out of my control.

I am not a superstar, nor a model, and certainly not a millionaire. My value is so much more than those assignations. I am a wife, a mom, a grandmother, an aunt, and one of four siblings, who I've come to value so much more at this point in my life. Fortunately, my story is not about dysfunctionality, abuse, or other heartbreaking stories we often hear about in today's society. My story is about love, tests, and experiences. My parents loved my siblings and me and instilled doing what is right in us, and we love them unconditionally. Being "governor and governess" over a modest, middle-class family, my parents worked hard and provided for their children the things we needed and often the things we wanted.

Today, I have to cherish all of my memories of my dad. He's gone now, but he instilled in us at an early age to love God, family, and country. His motto was, *'Treat people as you want to be treated,'* and that was the incipient indoctrination for my life and for my integrity. Unfortunately, in today's time, many people don't subscribe to principles like this, but, nonetheless, you learn to deal with these types of people. Honestly, dealing with these types of people disappoints me. In my opinion, it is so much easier to be happy, to have a positive outlook, and to look for the best in people even after you've seen the worst.

Life on My Own Terms

Living life on my own terms has not always been the case. There have been moments that I did not have a clear vision and I tried living someone else's vision for me. However, indulge me as I share some quick glances at defining times in my life, and perhaps you may see something that might relate to an event in your life. A few of these events now seem minuscule, but I assure you that at the moment they happened, I viewed them as monumental.

My early life was filled with involvement in all types of organizations. I enjoyed marching as a majorette, participating in girls' clubs, and playing softball. I especially loved softball (and still do), but my softball days were cut short when I was hit in the chest by a baseball bat. As a result, I was hospitalized, and my parents were probably shocked to find out that I had Sarcoidosis (an inflammatory disease that affects multiple organs in the body, but mostly the lungs and lymph glands). The diagnosis came in my senior year of high school. As a result, the baseball bat scarred enough tissue and gave this disease permission to enter into my 17-year-old body, mostly the lungs and lymph glands.

As a teenager, it did not faze me, and I enjoyed being at home out of school. When I returned to school, I immediately returned to everything with a vengeance. Up until a few years ago, when the Sarcoidosis started to raise its ugly head more frequently, I became acutely aware that something was seriously going wrong inside my body. I accept it as something I have to live with, since there is no cure for Sarcoidosis, but I do not take it for granted. Sarcoidosis can be life-threatening. However, I am determined to beat it, or at least keep it under control. Let me throw in this nugget for free. You can whine about what's going on in your life or you can get up and do something. My theory comes from one of my favorite movies, "Shawshank Redemption," in which Morgan Freeman states, *'You can get busy living or you can get busy dying.'* I believe that a person should fight as long as he/she has breath to fight. Nonetheless, there is more to come about Sarcoidosis later in this story. I simply wanted to set the stage for what I believe to have been my earliest life-defining moment.

Learning to Stand Up

A defining moment is when life forces a person to behave differently. I've had many defining moments and, looking back now, there were a few that could have gone in different directions. A moment that stands out is the occasion when I was preparing to graduate from Texas Southern University with my undergraduate degree. I was excited and full of energy. I still remember the day that I went to check the blackboard, the place where the names of graduates were posted – my name was not there. Shocked, I went to the registrar's office, confident that this was a BIG mistake. How could this have happened? Every semester I checked to ensure that I had completed all my academic requirements. Bam! I was told that I would not be able to "walk" because I was missing four credit hours. Imagine the emotions I felt? What was I going to tell my family? The invitations were already sent out, the guests were coming, and my parents were excited. Unbelievable!!! I had to either accept what was being said or stand up for what I knew was right. Later, I was informed that my rejection was related to my not taking a (PE) Physical Education class. *Thank GOD!* I thought, *I could easily explain why*, and presented my doctor's excuse. However, the registrar indicated that the university would not accept the letter that had been provided every semester at registration time. WHAT? She did not believe what I was saying or what the doctor had prescribed for my health over the many years. *Why was this information being provided two days before graduation?* At that moment, I could have thrown my hands up and declared that I quit. Do you know the stress of attending college and dealing with the high-powered, diverse personalities there? I came to the decision that I must stand firm and fight. Getting past the registrar seemed like an impossible task at the time. I refused to accept the response and fought for 48 hours all the way to the board of regents for the necessary signatures to override the registrar's decision. I "walked" and received my undergraduate degree. I do know people who left college and never returned because of something said or an incident so minor that could have quickly been resolved had they practiced a little more perseverance.

Perhaps, in today's society, younger adults might be more inclined to speak up. Still, in the 70s, not many 20-year-olds were willing to go up against the establishment, and especially, their university. Sadly, most would duck and run while wounded from the devastating words. Our emotions do play a massive role in our ability to make sound decisions. And, even today, 50-years later, I still get that same bubble in my stomach as I conjure up the courage to speak as I did then about injustice or about something as simple as calling when the trash is not picked up on a timely basis. We must find and keep our voice of reason optimistically and stand-up for what is right. Despite this incident, I am excited to tell you that I held no grudges, and the very next semester I returned and finally received my master's degree. This was the beginning of my learning how to deal with life's lessons.

Excited, Confused, and Transformed

As a newly minted college graduate, I was looking for a job that paid the BIG BUCKS. My part-time job at Shoppers Fair Discount Store was okay, but I wanted the big dollars. I applied with the FBI, Houston ISD, Houston Police, and the Houston Parks Department. A few weeks into the process, the Houston Park Police called and wanted to interview me. I was so excited but was secretly hoping that the FBI or HPD would call. After the interview, the very next day, I received the call that I would be hired as the first woman Park Police Officer. As a 92-pound, five-foot, one-inch young lady, I was going to be a certified Texas Commissioned Law Enforcement Officer. On top of that, my salary would be $322.00 bi-weekly, Hot-Diggity-Dog! I was going to be rich! Seriously, I had no expectations about this job, or the fact that I was the first woman to assume this position, let alone the fact that I was a woman of color joining the ranks of a new breed of women riding in police cars alongside our male counterparts.

The park police was established to cover the city of Houston's over-300 parks. Fresh out of the sheriff's academy, I witnessed and heard things that I had never experienced in all my 24 years. Wow! If folks only knew what was going on in the parks – everything from drugs to sex to kidnappings to murders – they would think twice before going there. This was a different and challenging time for me. The policemen were not happy about women joining their ranks, and in most cases, neither were their wives. My training officers were older, entitled white men who made it clear that they did not want a woman and especially a "colored" woman riding with them. I was scared and had to deal with the emotional turmoil that we all were going through. They didn't want me there, and most didn't care to know me. I did not know about discrimination, profiling, or sexual harassment. This was my first "real" job, and it was not supposed to be like this. I just needed to work. With God on my side, I pressed forward and worked hard to learn everything. I listened to what was being said, and more importantly, I refused to show my fears. This was a "must" in order to earn respect. In addition, I prayed the Serenity Prayer. It was my daily word. It helped get me through this testing time. It wasn't too long before I found myself being an accepted member of the team. I learned to chew Red Man tobacco, smoke cigars, and use colorful words. Even with this, I was – at most – liked by some and tolerated by others. Things were changing, and other women began joining the force of the predominately male profession. It was a nice feeling to know that I had proven that women could work alongside men and be equally as capable. I was a part of the change the world wanted to see.

I could see a transformation in me. I became more grounded, more confident, and more embedded into the organization. I became the "Go-to Person", a solutionist for questions, and a confidant to some for their concerns. I became the planner and executor for many departmental events. I was gaining trust and consensus among the officers and respectfully chosen as the elected leader and spokesperson. When I look back, I think, *What if I had given in to my fears? What if I had allowed the intimidation to get the best of me?* My hard work, faith, and wise approach allowed me to sit at the negotiation table with administrative leaders of the park police department, as well as with other organizations. Although my world was moving quickly and transforming before my eyes, I always kept humble, always trusted my "gut," and always remembered to maintain my humility. Repeating the Serenity prayer became my mantra. Standing my ground, standing up for what was right, became my method for affecting change.

Finding a Balance Between Work and Life

I met my first husband and the father of my son while working as a park officer. My then-husband was a Houston Police Officer. We had a good relationship, but it only lasted three years. We were blessed with a beautiful baby boy who has grown into the best son on this side of heaven, as well as a wonderful father, and an understanding husband. More importantly, he followed in his parent's professional path. He is a police sergeant.

Life is about growth, and there comes a time when you outgrow people for many reasons. I came across this quote on Facebook; *When you outgrow people, you will no longer be comfortable holding conversations with them nor being in their presence. Stop forcing it, you don't fit there anymore.'*

I realized at this intersection of my life that I was evolving. I was learning to speak my opinions and to stand my ground in spite of the fact that many didn't like this transformation. With a recent divorce and divided assets, a new future was ahead for me. It was time, AGAIN, to put on *my big-girl panties*. I could not lose focus nor be dismissive about life, because now, I had my son, my *little man,* to be a model for. I stood on the fact that God would place me where I needed to be, and the Serenity Prayer was with me. I knew the next stepping-stone would take me to a higher level.

My family and Park-Police friends were supportive, and my two best friends were ever ready to listen and help. Friendship is so valuable. These two ladies came to my rescue and were my sounding boards. Do you have a friend or two you can trust with your innermost feeling? If not, I strongly recommend that you build at least one trusting relationship. Everyone needs friends who will be around for the long haul. After defining moments, good or bad, you must move forward. Don't stand still.

Dismissing Naysayers

After several years on the force and in the capacity of a spokesperson negotiating change, I was amongst the leaders who were instrumental in advancing the Park Police, Airport Police, and City Marshall's to become members of the Houston Police Department Organization. What a day! Phew! Hard work, determination, and leadership do pay off. After being transferred to HPD, I had the opportunity to work with one of the assistant chiefs of police. This specific assignment became the learning ground that fostered my 36-year career. This is where I began discovering my significance. This was a new level of scrutiny, a higher standard of expectations and dedication coming from the seasoned HPD Officers who worked alongside me. It's hard to describe the excitement of being a member of the Chief of Police's Command Staff and working directly for the best (in my opinion) assistant chief.

I quickly recognized that I had the voice of the chief, the power of the chief's office, and the importance of the impact I could make. Of course, some individuals wanted to know how I got this job. After all, I came from the park police. I also wondered, *Why me?* There were moments that I felt that I was being tested to determine if I could deliver or if I would sink or swim? In these types of situations, I've learned that my humility, my work ethic, and my drive will not allow me to sink. I am always grateful for the opportunity to experience and face skepticism; these moments help me become stronger. The incredible thing about being misjudged or underestimated is that you can show people something different. It teaches you to work insanely harder, advantageously smarter, and with a direct purpose.

Over time, I learned that the department's leaders saw something in me that I had not seen in myself – Servant Leadership. The Leaders were willing to sponsor my continued leadership training wholeheartedly, such as training by Leadership Houston, Toastmasters, and the Bill Blackwood Leadership Command College hosted by Sam

Houston, Texas Woman's University and Texas A&M Universities. Additionally, I was appointed to various local and state boards. In time, my favorite chief left the department, and I was transferred to another Chief's office as the office manager. My reputation for my work ethic, leadership, accountability, and hard work preceded me.

After 18 years, I was still holding onto the Serenity Prayer. I began exploring new career possibilities. During this time, a friend called and said, 'The District Attorney's (DA) office is hiring investigators, are you interested?' I rushed over to the DA's office and picked up an employment packet. I returned it the next day. A week later, I was scheduled for an interview. Sounds familiar? Here we go again!

The Ultimate Crossroad

In April of 1993, I was hired by the Harris County District Attorney's Office (DA). Finally, I had hit the big times. Everyone in law enforcement knows the DA's office only hires the best of the best – the crème de la crème. Imagine the feeling when I was told to report to work on Monday, two weeks later. Also, a car would pick me up at 9 AM! What? A car coming to pick me up? I felt that I finally did it. But guess what? That bubble again formed in my stomach. I began to doubt this opportunity and my decision to leave HPD after 18 years. *What are you thinking? Why are you leaving?* These thoughts plagued me like a kid's first jump from a 20-foot diving board. It's not like I disliked my position. I wasn't leaving because the job position wasn't good but because I had grown, and it was time. Amelia Earhart says it best, *'The most difficult thing is the decision to act; the rest is merely tenacity. The fears are paper tigers. You can do anything you decide to do. You can act to change and control your life; and the procedure, the process is its own reward.'*

Again, I swallowed my doubts, started packing, and filing the necessary paperwork. My inner voice was telling me this was going to be good for me. With my hire, the DA's office had hired its first woman of color criminal investigator. Sounds familiar?

Working with a Passion

Before I share the fascinating journey of being a member of the DA's elite team, allow me to quickly tell you that in sixty-plus years of living and thirty plus years of public service, my life is filled with stories. And, I suspect that you too have a story to tell. Remember, as you go forward in your life's journey that you are creating a message that will help others. It's good food for the soul when you can relate your experience to someone else's.

Working with the elite of the elite at the District Attorney's office was just that, a fascinating journey. The office was a fabulous place, and of course, there were a few that were "all that and then some," but for the most part, it was a great place to work and equally great people. Nonetheless, with nice take home cars, perks, and glamour came deadlines and an excessive amount of work. When I would leave the office on Fridays for the weekend, my desk would be cleared free of cases. Nevertheless, on Monday, there would be a new pile of files that had come in over the weekend (criminals just don't stop). The role was very demanding! But, I loved the mystical awesomeness of being on the DA's team.

At HPD and during my time at the DA's office, I worked part-time at Miller Outdoor Theatre in a security role. Miller Theater became my home away from home. I had the privilege to work with all law enforcement agencies during my 30 years at Miller, from local police, FBI, Secret Service, and DEA, to Homeland Security. I loved Miller; I loved the people who worked there and patrons who attended the performances.

I was able to find love again while at Miller. This new guy (Kelly, aka Morgan) showed up to work for the theater. He became a good friend, someone I could talk to, laugh with, and we eventually became the best of friends. At the time, he had his own struggles and I had mine. He became my Knight in Shining Armor. And yes, several years later, he became my husband. Let me come back to our story. Miller was everything to me; it was the place where I would spend my summers. I would cook, bake, and on the Fourth of July, every police officer who showed up at the theater was welcomed to eat.

After 35 years, I walked away from Miller Theater to start two new adventures. I decided to return to school at the age of 54 to pursue a doctorate degree, my personal desire. I applied to Sam Houston University, was accepted, and the rest is history. I also joined my younger brother, in the direct sales marketing business for an energy company headquartered in Dallas, Texas.

During these years, my son had graduated from Texas Tech University. I married Kelly, my second husband, having thirty-seven of our close friends and family members celebrating with us at a beautiful location in Las Vegas. Kelly is a wonderful, caring man. Even with our ethnic differences, (by the way, Kelly is a Caucasian), he and I connected on all levels. Regardless of the chaos that surrounded us, we began to bond as a couple.

Like most families, we had our emotional challenges. We have worked and are continually working on building our relationship. *'Therefore, I tell you, whatever you ask in prayer, believe that you have received it, and it will be yours, Mark 11:24."* Since our marriage, we have grown together and have lost a few friends. They didn't say they were leaving, but we don't hear from them much anymore. And it's okay! Unfortunately, and most painful, we have lost interactions with Kelly's children. We miss them and hope they will call. That's another story.

Out the Door – A New Life

My new adventure with direct marketing (remember that I signed up with my younger brother) started matching my 36-years' retirement salary. So! A decision was made, after 36 years, I was retiring. *'Retirement means having the freedom to chase down your hopes and dreams and make them a reality.'* ~ *Anonymous* I'm going home to do what I want to do. I took a deep breath. I refused to look back as my co-workers stood at the top of the staircase, calling out my name and saying goodbyes. The tears formed in my eyes and rolled down my cheeks. It was bittersweet. I raised my hand and waved, never looking back. I ran to the waiting car.

Monday morning, April 4, 2011, three days into retirement, my dad calls my sister to say he wasn't feeling well. It was such a relief to no longer call for permission to go to the hospital to see what was going on with my dad. I often give credit to my energy business for allowing me to walk away from my career, but I know God has a way of making sure everything is in place for what is to come. My dad was diagnosed with Leukemia. He probably knew and just never told us. Weeks turned into months as we journeyed and sat with him from one hospital to another. Everyone in the family got involved. A few of the grandchildren learned things about their grandfather that they had not known, as well as things about the family. It still hurts me deeply even to reminisce over those days, but, sweet memories are priceless".

Life is really an adventure of doing the things that need to be done while enjoying the things that you want and love to do. I remain committed to working in the community, being a good servant, a good caregiver, and doing what I am guided to do by my inner voice. I do enjoy every moment of all of it. Earlier this year I became a member of Delta Sigma Theta Sorority at the age of 68. I am also in the process of learning to swim. I'm scratching things off my bucket list.

At the end of the day, we are all the same and we have three things in common, we are born, we live, and we die. It's the dash – that hyphen in between birth and death – that makes us different. These are the things that we should desire to be said as part of our legacy to our family, friends, and community. These are the things I'm certainly hoping to be shared about me when the time comes. As quoted by

Voltaire, *'The transformed soul asks what I can give to humanity rather than what can humanity give to us.'*

Meet Alessi Johnson

What are three words that best describe you?

Outspoken, Witty, Compassionate.

What is the biggest challenge you've ever faced in life?

Becoming homeless after first moving to another state.

Where do you find your P.O.W.E.R.?

I am often inspired by "my tribe," who are unknowingly a group of women that serve a purpose for being in my life. I have placed these women in this figurative group (in my mind) and they are ever-changing, and I do not close this group off to a certain number of women in my life. I believe people come into everyone's life for a reason or a season. Some of these women I have become empowered from have since moved on, but it makes room for new women to come into my life with different stories and backgrounds and with greater experiences to continue enhancing the strength that I need to act, to move, and to continue to inspire others.

Chapter 5

She Was Born: The Fibers that Created Her Being

Author: Alessi Johnson

"One of the hardest realities to the freest creatures of this planet, Is that we don't get to choose where we come from."

Alessi Johnson

It was a blessing to have grown up in a two-parent household and have my father present in my life. Although I lived with both parents, we weren't excluded from dealing with traumatic life events such as losing close family loved ones. Family deaths took a major toll on my parents as they attempted to deal with their hidden internal hurt while learning how to raise three girls as we aged and how to manage our household through it all.

I often would internalize my parent's emotional responses and actions displayed towards me during these difficult times thinking I'd done something wrong. I would feel as if they were angry with me, when really, they were processing and getting by as best as they knew how to do. When I would go to them for help or to seek counsel their response sometimes wasn't pleasant. As a young girl I was not accustomed to receiving such hurtful feedback. I felt these were personal attacks and I began to develop internal negative emotions.

I had so much love for my parents and I did not quite understand these new emotions that had begun to arise in me. Whatever those emotions were, it presented itself in the form of anger. Like any child growing up, I needed answers at pivotal moments in my adolescent life. My first heartbreak was when my father shut me down at the age of eleven because I wanted to know how to be a great friend to a guy at school. He heard me say the word "boyfriend" and internalized it as something totally different. This is when I built my first wall of defense. Unknowingly, my mother added to these insecurities and put a strain on our relationship just three years later when I was 14. It was during the time I'd hit a growth spurt and my body had begun going through changes that had resulted in me gaining weight. Her way of getting me to do something about it was in the form of tearing me down and calling me names. Insecurities about how I viewed myself had formed and I became silent.

These instances I experienced as a teenager with my parents played heavily into the way I began to view the world around me. From what I have come to learn, I now understand that it was not that my parents did not love me, it was just that they were doing what they probably witnessed their parents do when faced with adversity; push through. And because I was a child, I internalized their reactions towards me and associated how they felt about me with the emotion of anger.

Over the years of working in social services and as a part of my own healing process, I have learned that trauma does not always have to present itself in the form of tragedy and violence. Trauma can take on many forms and result in all parties affected by the trauma to become silent. My prayer is for this vicious cycle of silence to end in families, particularly, families of color. Learning that it is okay to speak about what hurts us while not feeling pressure to always keep things well-composed will bring all families of all backgrounds together.

Have you ever experienced trauma? What age were you? When the trauma you experienced first occurred, were you able to process what you were feeling?

Personally, I was not taught how to process my feelings. Therefore, it came out in unhealthy ways and resulted in my silence. Below I have listed some tips to help identify what you are feeling after enduring traumatic experiences.

Steps for Identifying How you Feel.

1. Allow the emotion you are feeling to have a voice.

Often, our first response to an unwanted feeling is to silence it for it to never be heard. DON'T! Allow the emotion you are feeling to have a voice. This can be in the form of screaming, talking, or simply writing the word that best describes your emotion on a piece of paper. Because once you see it. Once you hear it. It is going to make you want to do something about it. So, if it shows up again, you will already be able to voice that emotion.

2. Seek Counsel to Help Breakdown What you are Feeling.

One of the beauties of being born in a world full of people, is that we are not alone. In every person's life, stranger, or blood related, God places people in our lives who serve a certain purpose. For you, instead of people, it might be one person who you can go to in times of distress that is grounded and believes in a higher power that can help you. If you don't have that someone you can go to, I encourage you to go in prayer for God to send you someone you can seek counsel that has your best interest at heart and wants you to succeed. People like this are people I would consider to be in my inner circle. It is so important to have an inner circle because we all need someone to hold us accountable, to intercede in prayer on our behalf, and for support. To better help you identify who your inner circle might be, I have placed for you a chart you can use that will assist you.

MY INNER CIRCLE

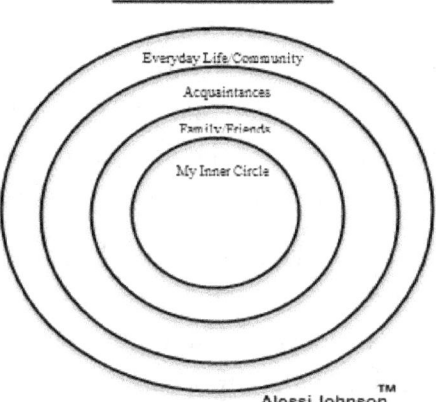

3. **Educate Yourself on your Emotion.**

Though you may seek counsel and you may have someone to talk to, it always helps to educate yourself on the emotion you are feeling. We have all been taught the basis of the everyday life emotions we experience since we were toddlers, however, the older we get, the more in depth the emotions' definition becomes. It is one thing to identify that you are angry, but it is another to discover the root to your anger.

4. **Pray.**

Simply put. Prayer changes things. Not only does prayer changes things, as you begin to mature your relationship with God, you will discover that having a prayer life and developing a personal prayer language will help you better deal with the many stressors of life. Prayer is also essential when identifying how you feel because there may come a time where you will have no one to talk to about the matters of your life and all you will have is the power of prayer. Remember, a prayer can serve as a weapon too.

The Painful Thorns from the Nest She Left

I had become so depressed that it began to weigh heavily on me. At the time, I was left feeling lonely. The two people who were always encouraging me, were there when I needed them, and were happy most of the time when we were together as a family had become unnoticeable to me. And because I was constantly ridiculed by my looks at school and having it being reinforced to me at home, I slowly began to isolate myself. I felt like the odd girl out. It was not shortly after that I learned about the "art of wearing the masks."

I was inspired to start living my life like the participants of a Mardi Gras parade. In some parades, the parade officials and even the participants of the parade are all wearing masks. Each mask can represent something different. Some masks are colorful. Some masks are that of someone smiling and others of someone frowning. However, the thing each person wearing the masks have in common is that you could not see the face of the actual person wearing the mask. I had thought to my fifteen-year-old self, *That's it! That's what I need to do.* I thought masking how I felt would help to keep anyone from noticing that I was depressed. So, I did just that. If I was sad, I would put on a happy face. If I felt like crying, I would make a silly joke so that whoever was around me would laugh. I had gotten so good at masking how I felt that in turn, people started gravitating towards me. I began to like this new feeling. It made me somewhat confident.

Before I knew it, I had lost who I was. I was blind to the significant changes I had made because I was so caught up in the unrealistic euphoria, I had created in my mind and was living in. Living in this state of mind was a coping mechanism for me. Being who I truly was and expressing how I really felt had brought me pain and grief but when I would put on my "other self," it worked, it disguised me, and it protected me.

By the time I started college, my mother had insisted I begin taking birth-control. Once I started taking birth-control, I started to lose weight. The downside is that my head went through the roof. While still acting as if I had my life together, the combination of a new slimmer body and my so-called persona was a dynamic duo from hell. I was a force to be reckoned with, with a one-way ticket down a dead-end street. Shortly after beginning birth-control, I became sexually active. Towards the end of my freshman year at college I had sexual intercourse with guys who only wanted me for just sex. My self-esteem was at an all-time low and I had felt so unworthy. I was angrier than I was at my family because this time, I had no one to blame but myself. After beginning having sex, it became an outlet for me yet left me feeling so empty. It was at this point that I had to take a step back before completely going over on the deep end.

One day while I was on campus, this young lady came up to me and handed me a flyer. It was for a local non-denominational church that was in town located not too far from the university's campus. My mother always told me that I can access God anywhere but it is better to worship together in the house of the Lord. I felt like since it was a church, it was a house of the Lord so to the church I went. When I began going, my life had begun to change. It was there that I had begun to learn about forgiveness and how to forgive. Though I was not in the spirit of forgiving, it was a start to me having a change of heart about things. The final semester of my freshman year of college was coming to an end. On the last day of my freshman year, I met a guy. Little did I know, this guy I was meeting would become my husband.

My husband and I started dating after that day. While dating my husband, I learned that he came from a hurt place as well. I later understood why we fell in love with each other. It was not because of love solely; it was because we were two hurt people and pain is what attracted us to each other. My husband was the first person who had seen me for me. He would tell me all the time, *'I see you.'* One day I was curious, and I asked him what he meant. He came out and told me that he knew I would put on fronts. He was the first person who saw through my mask. I asked him how he knew, his response was that he had worn masks too. After telling me this, I started to let my guard down. No masks. No fronts. Just me being myself. My husband joined me, and we started going to church together. This is when I began to expound upon the definition of forgiveness. I started to ask God now, what does the act of forgiving someone looked like. When I began to have a closer relationship with God, I was able to acknowledge that I was an imperfect human being that had been damaged and hurt. All along I was just an angry girl who wanted anyone that hurt me to feel the same pain or even worse than the pain they had caused me. I was living under this belief, but in my heart of hearts, my intentions are to hurt no one. It was not until I met my husband, another hurt individual, and being taught about God's saving grace that I learned it was okay to be broken.

Sometimes we can be so hard on ourselves. We tend to take the blame for the circumstances we are put in. We tend to blame ourselves for the abuses and inequities we have endured and instead of saying, 'Yes! This person or these people hurt me.' We stay silent. We try to remain poised while we are bleeding inside. I want you to know that it is okay for you to hurt. Give yourself the time and space to process.

Isolation for Preparation

Four years after dating my husband, we wed in 2013. After becoming married, I slowly began to lose sight of who I truly was as a person. I was so invested in being the best wife I could be, I was blinded at what was happening to me spiritually. One thing that brought me joy was getting a job in broadcast media as an on-air personality for a local radio station in the city in which we lived. I was elated because I felt like I was finally starting to make a mark with a huge opportunity in the field that I went to school for. Some say the first few years of marriage can be rough, and that it was for us. Our very first argument, turned physical leaving me with a bruised arm after having it slammed in a door. After this incident, I had done something that I was so used of doing, I had become silent. Because

I had never gotten into a physical altercation with a man before, I did not know what to call it. I am not sure if I was in complete shock or I was in denial. I had visited my parents and I wanted to tell them so bad but at the time I did not want to tell them out of fear of what my father might do to my husband. I finally had enough courage to tell my mother-in-law with whom I was close to and she was livid. She addressed my husband about it. Thinking back on it now, I should have taken the time to have both of us seek counsel because becoming physical is not okay.

We experienced extreme highs and extreme lows. And I did not have the time to process where we were in our marriage. Towards the end of our second year of marriage, I had to witness my husband go through a great loss. In April of 2015, my mother-in-law passed away from cancer. My mother-in-law's passing was hard for all of us, especially my husband. I had started working another job and had quit my radio job to support our household. It was a complete sacrifice for me, but I did not know what else to do. I was a young wife who had no clue how to be there for her husband. The events that took place after was like a ripple effect. We had moved to Dallas, TX three months after my mother-in-law's passing. My husband had a great job offer that would have put us in a better position financially. Before we moved, we found out I was pregnant with our first child. However, when we moved to Dallas, my husband did not take the job. I immediately became scared because this was my first pregnancy ever. And although my mother-in-law had passed, my mother was still here, and I felt like I needed her the most.

We started out living in and out of hotel and eventually moved into an apartment. After moving into our apartment, the car I owned was repossessed. Things started to go from bad to worse. I was taking taxis to my doctor's appointments up until I went into labor the following year and gave birth to our daughter. Giving birth to her was hard for me because I did not have my mother present. We were still struggling, and I had little time to heal. I was so exhausted because we were in a state away from our family and I had no help. I quickly became depressed. One day I ended up calling a suicidal hotline. I was not suicidal, but I wanted to throw my precious baby up against the wall. I knew something had to be wrong with me for me to even think of doing something like this. Shortly after this incident, I broke and told my parents. They put me and my daughter on the first flight home to Louisiana. It was there I received help to address post-partum depression. I eventually returned to Texas with a new mindset, a new cash car, and a job lined up for me.

After going back to work and starting a new membership at the YMCA, I began to grow bonds with new women I was meeting that were mothers and wives. These women helped to acknowledge that I was still depressed, they spoke words of encouragement over me, and they helped me to rise up!

For my 27th birthday, I took a trip to Austin, Texas with a young lady named Alma that was a part of my newfound tribe and we had the time of our lives. As we were touring the city, she brought me to this place known as the *"Wall of Graffiti."* Alma became excited about this place and the view before us because she is an artist herself. It was partly cloudy that day but still bright out. I had to shield my eyes to look at the top of the wall because it was so high. I opened my mouth and said, *'Wow, this wall is so high, you barely can see the top of it.'*

Alma looks at me and says, *'I know, let's climb to the top so we can have a better view.'*

I looked at her like I was crazy and said, *'DO WHAT?'*

She looked back at me and said, *'Let's climb it!'*

I started backing up pushing my hands forward and saying, *'Noooo, No, Can't Do.'*

Alma stops and with the calmest look in her eyes she says, ***'Take my hand.'*** I swear when she looked at me with her hand reached out,

I did not see Alma anymore, I seen the face of God using a soul to speak to me. I obeyed and grabbed her hand. I was hesitant at first, but I began to trust that we were going to make it to the top of that wall. Slowly the fear that I had started to fade because I began to believe. We made it to the top of the wall and boy, what a beautiful view it was. This manmade creation overlooked the city of Austin. I felt like I was on top of the world. When we made it to the top, I took a moment to view the city that looked back at me. As the wind started to blow through my hair, I declared that from that moment forward, I choose to choose me.

This was more than just a trip for me, it was a defining moment in my life that helped me to make a shift in things. After having to deal with loss. The loss of a woman I considered my second mother, losing my vehicle, and leaving my hometown; yet, welcoming a new life all at the same time made me exhausted. I felt like I was left stuck with the inability to use my God given gift he gives to every woman to birth things into the atmosphere. At this time, I was unable to identify who I was and own my newfound responsibility of who I had become. But this beautiful moment on the hilltop of that wall that day was my first reminder of who I am.

Often as women, we put ourselves last after taking care of everyone else around us. Do not be afraid or feel guilty for taking time out for your own self-care. It is okay to choose to take care of yourself.

When She Let Go, She Transformed

Every woman has her beauty marks.

You need adversity to come into your wisdom.

It is up to us to transform it.'

Jada Pinkett Smith

I returned from my birthday trip transformed with a renewed mindset. It was at this point I started to reevaluate some things in my life. Fighting so hard to regain a sense of myself. I realized that I had to take a step back.

Though we had major setbacks, things finally started going in the upward direction financially for us. However, enough had become to be enough after I discovered my husband was using my debit and credit cards to gamble. I had begun hiding my wallet. One day, my blood pressure had become elevated and I felt like I could not breathe that I went into the E.R. It was because I was under pressure and stressed out beyond measure. After all the events and going to the Emergency Room, I stopped and asked myself a series of questions, *What the hell am I doing?* and *Is staying in this marriage even worth it? Is this how love is supposed to feel? Is this love?* After a long talk with myself and prayer. I did what most women would not do. I separated from my husband.

I started to see a counselor. In counseling, this is where I learned about verbal abuse. I also learned that it is just as worse than physical abuse. I had an awesome counselor. One thing that I found interesting about my time in counseling is that after the first session, we no longer talked about my husband. I was forced to talk about myself. At the time, I was so consumed with my role as a wife and a new mother, that I did not even think much of myself to even talk about myself. But it was also here that my healing began.

I had to go as far back as to my childhood. I had to go back to my eleven-year-old self and address the first time my heart was broken by my father. I had to address my fourteen-year-old self and go back and forgive my mother. Towards the end of my counseling sessions, I had finally begun the process of forgiving. I forgave my mother and father. And I forgave myself. My actions and how I acted towards my family were not a reflection of the love I have for them including my sisters.

I ultimately shunned my family in search for love thinking I was being loved.

I have since began the process of forgiving my husband as well. After a year and half of being separated from my husband, we attended marital counseling. We briefly reconciled, but now our divorce is being finalized. I now know what I want and what I will not accept. I can walk away knowing I did everything I could to make my marriage work. I have also found my voice and have gained an inner strength that I always possessed but had not utilized and it feels good!

Steps to Knowing When to Let Go

1. Is This Situation Causing Me Anxiety/Stress?

Going back to the beginning of this chapter, I gave you steps on how to identify your feelings. Using the same techniques from the steps on acknowledging how you feel can be a great tool to use when answering this question. If the answer to this question that your life's obstacle is a part of your stressor, it is an indicator that your situation is not healthy for you which may be a cause for you to let it go. Remember! *'Your peace is all you may have at times. Protect it at all cost!'*

2. Will Staying in This Situation Hinder or Help Me?

Often when we as women find ourselves in situations, we already know that staying in the situation will more than likely hinder us, yet we stay anyway. Stop! It is so easy to stay but perfecting your prayer language and leaning not to your own understanding will allow you to be able to make the best decision for your life.

3. What is the Worst That Can Happen If I Leave The situation I Am In?

Sometimes leaving may or may not always be an option for you when letting go. Letting go can come in all shapes and forms. One of the best forms of letting go is letting go of a situation in your mind. Once one let go of what they cannot control, often they come out with a victory because it means that their obstacle has not defeated them. If you can leave, what will that picture look like? Will it be bad, or not so bad after all? And if your situation is not something that requires you to leave, yet it is a situation you need to let go. Ask yourself, 'What is my last straw?' If you have reached your, *"last straw."* Ask yourself, 'Why am I still here?'

If you have found yourself in a situation like mine. Now is your time to **speak!** Bring forth those things that are not pleasant to you and open your mouth about it. We were not built to hold everything in. If you are pretending to hold yourself together while you are walking through the toughest storm of your life, it is only going to work for so long. For me, it took me going back to the root of the problem and acknowledging the root no matter how ugly it was, or the people involved. This might be the same for you. The great thing about God and his saving grace is that he is equipped to fight our battles. Going through challenging experiences have forced me out of my once silent self. My prayer is for you to find your inner strength and use your voice to break your years of silence too.

Meet Nkia Haughton

What are three words that best describe you?

Versatile, Courageous and Fun-loving.

What is the biggest challenge you've ever faced in life?

The ability to forgive and move on from my past was my biggest challenge in life. This cycle was a holding pattern captive of my emotional and mental freedom. I over came by discovering my identity through the profession of my faith in God. My faith gave me the strength to forgive and move on from my past.

Where do you find your P.O.W.E.R.?

I have found "POWER" through prayer and my relationship with God. How? Resting on God's word allows me to rejuvenate mentally, emotionally, and spiritually. This found freedom allows me to be fully grounded in my roles as a wife and a mom.

Chapter 6

From Trauma to Triumph

Author: Nkia Haughton

In our society there are a few cultural norms as it pertains to the ideology of what family life should "look" like. In sequential order, a healthy baby is born, the baby grows up happy in a stable and conducive environment and becomes a self-sustaining adult. The adult gets married and has a family of their own thus starting a generational cycle of a coveted dynamics that incorporates passing down preconditioned notions of a myriad of concepts. All the ideologies above are good grounded desires to have. However, realistically, life experiences whether past or present are not like this for everyone especially in today's society. Far too many of us have encountered an experience that has molded our perception and responses on the contrary. Due to unforeseen circumstances that life may bring, this is not a testament of all of mankind.

Although I will be sharing some of my most tragic life moments with you, I understand the value of tapping into your power and finding your voice. I was raised in the Caribbean, surrounded by beautiful water, warm days and calypso music. The Caribbean is the place that many people visit when they want to escape from the troubles of life and find peace. As a young girl, the life I experienced was the opposite of this scenario. Up until the writing of this book I have not shared most of my traumatic experiences. Today, thankfully

I am free from the stigma and negative mindsets that can invade the life of a woman who encounters tragedy, repeatedly, at such an early age. As I share my testimony, I want you to not see me as a victim but as a woman of God that has endured, overcome and become a champion for the voiceless.

At the age of five the physical abuse started. The memories of what I had to endure left me traumatized for most of my childhood into adulthood. I was physically, verbally and sexually abused by family members that I trusted and loved. It was like a horror movie, being slapped so hard that my face would twist to the other side and being punched in my side until I lay gasping for breath. I was often devalued and rejected. I was demoted and dehumanized by relatives replacing my given name with the word "thing" when calling or addressing me, often labeling me as retarded. There were many other traumatic moments that I encountered that were pivotal and breaking points in my life but I have decided to share my experience with you on how I have endured being molested and finally living a life with an identity through a discovered purpose. From the outside looking in if I was reading this, I would be irate too but would also have a bunch of questions, the first being, who did this to you?

Sadly, the abuse was caused at the hands of relatives. I remember laughing and playing hide and go seek in groups that included this relative on numerous occasions. He used this opportunity to touch me inappropriately on my private parts. Eventually he would molest me repeatedly and threaten me that If I told my parents he would take me away. As a five-year-old this was very frightening not knowing what to do or how I could have found a way to make it stop. I begged him to stop, but when I started to cry, he would turn the background music up loud enough to drown out my voice or place his hand over my mouth.

For years I did not have any interest in socializing with anyone. I would go straight to my room when I arrived home from school and

I took an interest in playing with my pets or toys instead of the neighborhood children. The straw that broke the camel's back and affected my moral long-term was the day the molestation was discovered and how it was handled. One-night a relative spent the night at our house. My father worked late at nights and my mom went to college so to assist with childcare provisions we often went by our family members or family members stayed by us. After my cousins and siblings went to bed this defiling individual came to me and forced himself on me. I was mortified and scared all at the same time. I went from the innocence of playing with dolls to being conscious of my body, completely ignorant at the tarnished functions of my body parts. While all of this was going on, he had his hand pressed tightly covering my mouth. When he was done, I was instructed not to say anything and he threatened to take me away from my parents if I did tell.

After violating me, there I laid with no clothes on and my mom walked in and caught him in the act of getting dressed. Immediately, she started sobbing. Once my other family members came, I got snatched and dragged away and was beaten in my head with shoes, slapped so hard, my face twisted, bitten about my body, called names like slut and a hoe. My father came with his gun and shot at him with the intent to kill him but missed. I was yelled at in the process citing that it was all my fault (I was just 6 years old) even though the person involved was a teenager!

After this ordeal, my happiness was nowhere to be found in my life for years and I became completely isolated and did not talk to anyone. I felt like I let my family down and at the same time I felt violated and confused. The seed of feeling the need to protect and take care of myself was planted and it grew extremely high walls around my heart. I went through silent hell! Because of this, I conditioned my mind into a state of nonchalant peace. Peace in a manner of existing and not living. I was bent on refusing to let anyone too close to my heart.

At times there was inner conflict because ignoring or not knowing how to handle situations in life can be detrimental. Keeping things in and not dealing with it is ineffective. This was the lesson I learned through my persecution. I mentally created a bubble around myself and conditioned my mind to sweep the trauma underneath the rug. I did not want to face my reality or deal with the circumstances. A transient like state was my counterfeit haven for a false sense of peace and stability.

There was a heavy burden on my shoulders, and a dark shadow was cast upon our home. My parents who were once so in love with one another became engulfed in the ordeal and regularly found themselves arguing. I witnessed the guilty look in their faces when they looked at me as if it was their fault that it had happened to me. My father, the strong man who was like a giant in my eyes, would weep like a baby. The aroma of frustration grew thick in our household. The love quickly began to escape, and I felt unloved and unwanted. One day, I just could not take it anymore and I grabbed a knife and started yelling at my parents to stop arguing. I wanted to end my life, but just as I went to stab myself in the stomach my father pried the knife out of my hands and hugged me tight.

I am so glad my father intervened that day. I know that my life has a meaning, and my prayer is that I can help save other children's lives. My advice to parents or any person dealing with a similar situation is to pay attention to who is watching your child and pay attention to the signs your child is displaying. Make sure that whoever is the "responsible party" for providing care has your child's best interest at heart. I believe in the importance of children recognizing parental guidance as one of authority. However, there must be a balance. Authority alone is not enough. Authority balanced with nurturing, sense of love and compassion, and open communication will build a stable relationship. I know firsthand as a mom I push my emotions aside in order to keep an open mind. It is important for me to be very inviting in a responsive tone and approach so in the long run my child will feel like we can talk about anything.

On the contrary, if we do not consistently overreact or do not develop these communication skills, we as parents ought to be careful not to subconsciously push kids away as a means of disinterest or frustration. Take time for them, do not tell them to sit down to shew them away. Also, your kids should be one of your top priorities. Recognize that maintaining their spiritual and social growth is vital. On the flip side, involving yourselves in natural activities is equally as important. All these provisions and working towards it is indeed important. However, do not let the lack of time and attention be filled by activities or persons (distractions or negative connotation) that fuel them to ultimately gain their attention if not now in the future from unproductive sources.

Play is important! Kids naturally play to learn and connect and observe the real world through make- believe. When they imagine, it gives them hope to where they would like to be when they grow up. It allows them to imagine the responsibility they would have to encounter as a mother, father, man, or woman. There should be an obligation to help and be what our family needs and provide for our household. Parents are role models and the only perfect being outside of this world is Jesus.

When kids act up do not be so quick to counteract chastisement, why of course being rude and disrespectful is not acceptable but find out "why." Get to the root of the behavior. Kids need to feel that their presence in the family is equally as important and not just there for mommy and daddy to take care of them. They have even greater responsibility especially in today's world to find their place in society and lift up a standard. Please do not talk down to your kids. Instead speak words that spark hope and courage. Proverbs 22:6 says, 'Train up a child in the way he should go; even when he is old, he will not depart from it.' Ephesians 6:4 says, 'Fathers, do not provoke your children to anger, but bring them up in the discipline and instruction of the Lord.' Kids are not to be placed in a mold. They are to be shaped by God's intended purpose for their lives along with the cultivation of their talent's insights. Take care of them, cherish them.

Do not allow them to be placed in vulnerable situations. I know you cannot be everywhere all at once. The one thing that you can ensure to the best of your ability as a parent is your ability to pray consistently covering them in your prayer and installing principles. God is everywhere. Place them in the hands of God and leave them there! Whatever you teach them you must be the example in the home. Doing contrary sends a conflicting perception to a child who already has the task of deciphering theory to the practical principle. Having a child is a privilege not a right. It is a full-time responsibility! I love you can never be said too much. Do not rear kids with a mindset to prove themselves to you. Instead, let them live up to the standards you have taught in the home. One moment can lead to a lifetime of change for the good or the bad. Do not allow bad cycles to linger. It is one thing to push your kids to incite but more effective to be a part of the change to bring about change. Words have power even if it's casual to call children names outside of their given name. Never chastise a child out of frustration, this is subliminally sowing seeds of discourse when children must handle challenging situations if not now in the future.

As an adult having had experienced trauma it left negative effects on my character, choices, and habits in my life. I had a lot of bitterness, I was short-patient and angry, especially when a conversation was perceived as critical or judgmental or when my input was not valued. This anger often surfaced in my work and professional relationships. I took everything personal. It took a lot for me to get over myself and allow people the opportunity to offer their constructive criticism. It often would cause an inner conflict because I knew I did not need any affirmation from anyone.

Months passed and I found myself in an environment that was conducive to me coming out of my shell. Our church had a youth program that I remember I thoroughly enjoyed. It was like a breath of fresh air, a way of escape, and something to do where I can come out of my regular element to seek help I needed to deal with the post-traumatic stress. Don't keep your emotions bottled like I did for years. This is your God given human right to express yourself. Cry and/or be vocal in your communicative efforts. Only the Lord can bring this kind of revelation, healing, and restoration enough so that I am able to talk about it freely. My body aged but my mentality was stunted in growth. So, in other words I physically experienced these cycles but hindered the integration of "coming into my own."

Children are discovering their surroundings and sense of self. I was robbed of this stage; I basically grew myself up mentally and emotionally. The psychological effects lingered for a long time. In my world I was all alone. My world was a very cold dim place. I lacked the maturity because it hindered my willingness to evolve as a person. I was stuck on a level that I felt I grasped control! My depression held me captive so much to the point I would have social anxiety. I did not know what "normal" was and as cliché as it may seems it was the truth. I never experienced normal…normal in my view back then was seeing the other children who were untouched and actively social with the other kids and/or their family. I do remember as a child envying the perception of what balance looked like.

Dreams, goals, or common interests dwindled to low or no enthusiasm. I acknowledged my parents but became a little distant because I had a feeling of letting them down. I was bad with my rationale behind accepting improper treatment. Rejection was nothing new under the sun because I experienced this in school. There was absolutely no one that I had that I felt that I could have talked to. I even began to pray to die. I questioned God, the God I learned about in church as to why he sent me to this world. I didn't blame Him. Even though I was young, I was just hurt and searching for answers as to how and why at such a young age these things were happening to me.

If you have a child that has been molested in any way, I suggest you as a family get counseling. Counseling is good because it gives you a different perspective on dealing with the grief. In my era seeing a counselor was acquainted with being for a person who has a mental disorder. This is completely opposite in nature. Everyone can use a counselor to help them through their process. They listen without having any bias opinion. They are more prone to telling what you need to hear and not want to hear. Their emotions are not attached to you and can provide advice with a clear mindset. You might feel more comfortable opening up. Counseling comes in so many different options. You can visit a psychologist, pastor, Christian counselor, or Elder in the church. The individual must be the one to come to the realization that they need help. Pretending that nothing happened or unwillingness to receive help will never bring closure. The quest for sound counseling should be an objective. Some people deal with frustration by "sweeping it under the carpet". Avoidance of a life changing ordeal is detrimental to the individual's mental health. Our progress in life is based on our search. A child world belief system views concept is important. It should be a duty to try and gage or steer them back to recovery and further quest on a path of discovering their purpose or destiny.

Being Restored

An attempted rape was the beginning of my restoration process. I remember closing my eyes and asking the Lord to fight for me to help me out of this situation. Psalm 46:1 says, 'God is our refuge and strength, a helper who is always found in times of trouble.' Within seconds he stopped and walked out of the room… I cried my eyes out and sat distraught on the floor trying frantically to pull myself together. I remember gasping for breath in fear and brokenness. Memories of past ordeals began to surge in overdrive mentally. I remember shaking because I was so afraid, angry, and hurt all at the same time. I wondered, *Why me and when will all this end?* Time after time at this moment I was fed-up with the turmoil that infiltrated my life and I yearned for it to stop!

I can definitively say that for a change to occur we have to be willing to do our part to bring about change. In my hurt, I was also enraged with a will to change the course of my life. I had flashbacks throughout my history. Finally, I remember standing up and proclaiming with trust in God that would never happen to me again. My fighting back was not so much retaliation but my will to win and see a positive change.

One day I chose to forgive and let go all the bitterness that was in my heart. To date I do not have any more animosity towards those that violated me. Arriving at this point was not easy but the freedom I have now is worth it. After processing my healing I learned:

1. Do not stay in any environment that does not promote peace or give you a freedom to bask in the quality of life.

2. Stop apologizing for things that are beyond your control. I had a habit of saying sorry for everything.

3. It's okay to get help! I cannot emphasize this enough. Go to counseling or seek assistance from organizations specific to your crisis. Take some of the weight or burdens off your shoulder that life brings and go vent to someone that has the training or skills to help you. Do not sit there and wallow in self-pity! I have found that it's better to talk to a stranger or someone that is not emotionally attached to you because the advice 8 times out of 10 will be sound judgment and not an emotional plea.

4. Increase your self-worth. Challenge yourself to grow and evolve. You deserve better. Do not give anyone or anything power over you to the point where you remain stagnant. At

the end of the day this is your responsibility. God always makes ways out of no way, so you will always have hope to overcome. Do not get complacent or comfortable. Always strive to better yourself.

5. Your pain is wrapped in your purpose. Find whatever that is and make a difference for others with a similar situation. You can volunteer at different organizations rendering your talents or write a book. Everyone has a story and there is someone waiting out there that needs to hear yours to impact their life.

6. Love yourself first and see yourself as deserving of your desires. Love on yourself. Get your hair done, manicure, pedicure, etc. Be the best you that you can be in your mind, body and soul.

7. Break the cycle. Do not pass the insecurities on to your children. Do not pass your fears or bad habits on to your kids. Be the living example of the principles that you teach your children.

8. Change the habits in your life that are unproductive. Do not procrastinate. Before you know it, time will slip away. Focus and engage yourself on achieving goals and aspirations. Be practical and noticeably clear by writing down your vision and what it takes to achieve them.

When I met my husband, who is a military man, he had a huge battle to fight – *figuratively*. Which war was this? Me, yes I confess. My body had aged, but my mind was in limbo due to past experiences. The transition from being single to married life was not an easy task. So how did I overcome the residual challenges and conflicts from my past? I had to slowly let my guard down and remove the walls that kept everyone out. I had to learn how to trust and love. God gave me the perfect person, and he was very careful with how he dealt with me. Whenever we spoke it was pure conversation or jokes at the time;

and never anything physical. He was a Godly man and he prayed for me and with me. Even to this day I have never had to demand respect or ask to be treated like a lady with him. I know this is not the case with most women who have been abused. They find it hard to open themselves to the possibility of being loved. I had to learn not to push true love out of my life. I had prayed for true love, so when he showed up, I had to be willing and open to do the work.

If you know that you want to be in a good relationship you must resolve your biggest self-issues. Take as less "baggage" as possible to a long term committed relationship. Beyond appearance or material things ask yourselves is this person the right fit for me? Does he support your goals? Is he sensitive to your needs? Does he exemplify the level or has the potential to show the level of compassion that you need? If yes, how does his principles and values connect with yours? These are all questions you will need to ask yourself.

When I was blessed with a husband God showed me, he was a bonus. He did not bring love to my life; it was already there. He taught me how to love, break down barriers, and restored my mindset towards the opposite gender. My advice for those contemplating marriage or have been victims of abuse is listed as follows:

- Prince charming does not exist! Using the laws of attraction is a vital role but more so with the individual's willingness for stick-ability in the relationship.

- I do not believe in falling in love (infatuation). I believe in growing to love an individual through learned experiences.

- My husband and I mutually agreed to not keep any secrets that had a potential of negatively impacting our marriage.

- Get pre and post marriage counseling.

- During frustrating circumstances do not resolve the conflict by reacting on the impulse of experience.

- Learn to let things go…don't harbor hurt or pain in your heart.

- Be respectful and sensitive to each other's needs and show compassion.

- Don't allow your significant other to pay for other's mistakes.

Marriage is an investment! You will only get out of it what you sow into it. I love you is not measured only in words but by actions. Keep maintaining yourselves as an individual e.g. get your hair done, medical checkup, me time etc. for you will not be "good" to serve your family or kids if you are not good to yourself.

Finally, when I had my son, I was all in for he completely stole my heart. The instant bond we shared caused me to realize that he will not "pay" for my past. I am committed to loving him unconditionally and allow his home to be the example of a well-balanced environment. While it is important to pray it is also important to omit habits that influence bad generational cycles.

As I close if you are or know someone who is a victim of abuse; today I urge you to get help, this is how I was able to move on with my life. With God in your life you build the courage enough to go against the tide and live with an understanding of purpose. You do not have to deal with life and the troubles of life alone. The "ball" has always been in your court to live out or strive for the life you desire to succeed.

Know that you are special, significant, and strong enough to come out of your trials in life as a winner! The fact that you survived you can make an impact in the lives of others. Someone is waiting and needs to hear your story. Only you can determine the magnitude of what making a difference means to you. Shake off the mindset of sorrow and defeat. Be courageous and determine that those days are done. Think positively and hope for the best. Set goals for your life and write them down. Learn how to encourage yourself! This is important in your progression. Do not stay in the immediate environment of anyone to down talk to you or anyone to inflict abuse. Surround yourself with "leaders" via books, social media, mentors etc. to develop your goals.

My hope for everyone reading this is for you to live a fruitful life. May contentment, love, joy, peace, and happiness fill your hearts and mind. Rebuilding requires patience and consistency with your endeavors. Things do not always happen overnight. The expectation of healing and restoration does not suggest that the turmoil of experience did not happen to you. It simply is a changed state of mind, meaning it no longer rules your emotions. I cannot stress this enough, Get help! There are organizations in place to help you. Do not fall into the trap that you are all alone because you are not! Moving forward speak positively, no more excuses. No more woe is me or sympathy-imposed aggression. Looking back receiving sympathy played a part in being a therapeutic crutch that enabled me to stay in the mindset of existing and not living. There is a misconception that other individuals who are at the stage of where you want to be, have it all together. Also, it is so easy to look at the world around you and feel as if you "want the experience" of visual perceived happiness through the lives of others. Well, guess what? No one lives a perfect life, everyone goes through something that places them on an emotional roller coaster. What makes individuals win is a determination and passion to achieve against all odds to get to the other side or "through". Every step you take in strides is advancement towards your future. You are a winner and have what it takes to make it! Cheers to a new beginning as your future is bright.

Meet Sandra Heard

What are three words that best describe you?

Loving, Driven and Faithful.

What is the biggest challenge in life you've ever faced?

The biggest challenge I've ever had to face was the decision to stay or leave my marriage after the Lord exposed my husband's secrets including betrayal. His behavior and a myriad of other things led to a 15-month separation during the sixth year of our marriage. Those dark times were full of heartache, pain, and despair that resulted in bitterness and resentment that I allowed to take root in my heart unknowingly.

Where do you find your P.O.W.E.R.?

First and foremost, I get my "POWER" through my faith in my Lord and Savior Jesus Christ. I love to worship the lord, I love to sing and I enjoy spending quiet time in prayer, reading and studying the word of God (bible) and through journaling. I also draw strength from my husband because of our close relationship and I love how we pray together and when he covers me in prayer.

The Power of Forgiveness: The Key that Unlocks the Door to Freedom

Author: Sandra Heard

As a young child desperately longing for my mother's attention, love, and affection; I remember sitting on the stairs one evening staring at her after she'd come home from a long day at work and I thought to myself, *That's not my mom, that's an Alien!* She was just too tired to meet the needs of her young daughter. This made me question if my own mother loved me. While she loved me as best she knew how, it wasn't enough for the little girl that was already developing a lot of hurt and pain deep on the inside. Not just from feeling unloved by her mom, but the longing for a father who was absent because he was dead and buried six feet underneath the ground!

I often wondered if my mother loved me because I never heard the words "I love you" while growing up nor did she show much love and affection. At least the way I needed and desired it. Those are some of the most important attributes a child needs from a nurturing mother. The mothering style I received while growing up is referred to as the *Phantom Mom* according to Dr. Henry Cloud & Dr. John Townsend, authors of *The Mom Factor*. The Phantom mom is one that is *not* emotionally available for her children. Instead, she meets their physical needs like food, shelter and clothing. Thus, her children don't receive their five basic needs including safety, nurture, basic trust, belonging and someone to love.

As equally important is the role of a father in the life of his daughter. He was created to protect, provide, and show her how a man should love and treat a woman. Having an absent father caused a lot of pain and unknowingly left the wounded little girl trapped inside of me. I had no idea those temper tantrums displayed as an adult in times past was my inner child I never knew existed prior to healing. The devastating effects of my unmet needs left feelings of abandonment and rejection that resulted in a wounded heart and low self-esteem.

For many years, I felt unattractive. I didn't like my God given features including my lips and nose. I thought they were both too big so I wore fake (nonprescription) glasses and sat them on the tip of my nose thinking they would make me more attractive. Instead, I looked more hideous. I even thought my skin was as dark as the asphalt on the ground based on the number of times I heard, 'You are so pretty to be dark.' I often said to myself, *Why can't I just be pretty?* Those were some of the lies I believed for a long time.

How many of you can relate to my childhood pain? Have you ever felt unloved, abandoned, or rejected? Those ill feelings was the start of a shattered and broken little girl that blossomed into a shattered and broken woman scarred with emotional wounds that I had no idea existed until the dark secrets were exposed in my marriage. Because of my inadequacies, I didn't realize those ill feelings buried deep inside of me were like magnets attracting people with similar issues. I was attracting other hurt people. Did you know that hurt people – hurt other people?

Patterns in Relationships

Unbeknown to me those feelings of abandonment and rejection would soon spiral out of control and lead to the *little girl* inside of me crying out and looking for love in all the wrong places! I continuously allowed myself to be subjected to pain, betrayal, abuse in some cases and even neglect. It became apparent I wasn't a good judge of character that resulted in a seventeen-year span of one bad relationship after another. From what I recall, it started at the age of ten when my step father almost stole my innocence. My longing for a father made me the perfect target. I was so excited when my mom told us she was getting married. From the moment he moved into our home, I started calling him daddy. We got off to a great start until the day he had me lay on top of him and placed my hand on his private area. I immediately felt uncomfortable and thought to myself, *Something is not right*. I never went back around him after that day. I was afraid to tell my mother so I held onto that secret until I became an adult. I was already struggling with trust issues and that made things worse.

In my quest for love, I met a young man who had a major impact on my life. I fell in love with him, but for the wrong reason. I was fifteen and half years old at the time and he was seventeen. I took an initial interest in him only to get back at a friend who was also attracted to him that betrayed me in times past. My so call revenge resulted in teenage pregnancy. I never thought that would happen to me. Yes, the first time I gave myself to that young man, I became pregnant. A week later I was expecting my menstrual period and it never came. How was I going to explain it to my mother? I was already afraid of talking to her. My mom told me not to have sex, but she never shared the responsibility of such an adult act between a husband and wife. Or, the consequences that can result when you have sex outside of marriage like an unwanted pregnancy. What's crazy is that I got advice from my teenage friend who was sexually active during that time. She told me the best time to have sex is a week after your ovulation.

Wrong answer! In fact, that's the worse time to have intercourse since it's the most fertile time for females to become pregnant once they've started their menstrual period. Apparently, that was not sound advice. Unfortunately, that's what teenagers do especially if they're afraid to talk to their parents including something horrific as rape.

I'll never forget the time I was date raped by a man I was acquainted with. I was infatuated with him because he was handsome. He worked in a hair care store not too far from where I attended college. I would drop in from time to time to see him. We had exchanged numbers and talked on the phone sometimes. I thought there was a mutual interest between us. One evening, he offered to drive me home and that's when it happened! I had on a long tan skirt that day. We started kissing and before I realized what was happening, he held me down and raped me! I was devastated by what happened! I said to him, 'You Raped Me?'

His response, 'It's my word against yours. You came with me willingly.'

I felt helpless and ashamed! I carried that pain around for years without realizing it. I suffered in silence. Have any of you ever suffered in silence? I even blamed myself for what happened because I kissed him willingly. But, I wasn't trying to be intimate with someone I was still getting to know. Truth of the matter, many men I liked and/or dated in times past thought I would be easy since I already had a child. Ironically, some men wouldn't date me for the same reason. The residue of his behavior made it more difficult for me to trust men.

For a long time, I felt I had divulged too much personal information entirely too soon with someone I barely knew. I felt it made me a target for him. Women, how many of you have shared too much personal information with men you hardly knew and later found yourself being hurt and/or taken advantage of? If they are not men of integrity, they will take advantage of you. I believe it all points to low self-esteem or not understanding your worth. When you don't know your self-worth and/or don't respect yourself, men won't respect you either. Unfortunately, we need discernment and know how to be a good judge of character which I lacked in those days. I began to notice a pattern of unhealthy relationships. Essentially, I kept dating the same man except they each had a different name. But, who was the common denominator? Me! Unfortunately, I didn't notice this until after I met the man of my dreams.

The Man of My Dreams

After meeting the man of my dreams, my life turned upside down! I was the wife of a Godly man. The one who was specifically chosen for me, yet there was so much turmoil between us that I felt was all a farce because I thought the God I serve would not dare allow this to happen to me! Oh what a tiny web we weave when we think more highly of ourselves than we ought to! That was me after accepting Jesus Christ as my Lord and Savior and during the time I began to mature spiritually. That self-righteous attitude got me in a lot of trouble and the Lord knew exactly what was needed to bring me to my knees.

The year that shook me at my core and brought me to my knees was the summer of 2008 after the dark secrets in my marriage started to unravel! My perfect little world came crashing down leaving me alone to face the aftermath of my husband's betrayal. My need for healing became evident. I was full of poison and experiencing the side-effects of unforgiveness because I was focused on the hurt and pain caused by my husband's betrayal. Side-effects are ill feelings of anger, bitterness, and resentment to name few. This was a rude awakening that took me by storm!

Desperate for change, I prayed and cried out to the Lord daily. He began to peel me like an onion one layer at a time. Those negative emotions hidden in my heart left me teary eyed with disbelief. Prior to the exposure of betrayal, the Lord had given me a sneak peek through dreams. While I asked God what He was trying to show me, deep down inside I didn't want to believe my husband was cheating on me. Ironically, the red flags were staring me in the face, but I wasn't ready to deal in truth at that time. I had been wearing a mask for so long and accustomed to saying what many Christians say when hurting and not operating in truth, 'I am blessed.' Or some people say, 'I am highly favored and blessed in the Lord or blessed by the best' when deep down inside they are hurting just like some of you. Unfortunately, those are not words that describe how someone feels. Instead, they are mere words of expression that I refer to as a cover up when people are not ready to face the truth and work on their issues.

Have you ever felt hurt and wondered why? Perhaps it's those issues you buried deep inside thinking they would just go away over time. Not facing the truth or dealing with hurt and pain can be more damaging than you realize. People who wear masks never reach their full potential because they are carrying around dead weight that can erupt at any moment! Negative emotions bottled up inside typically explode when we least expect it, because we've learned how to master hiding behind our issues. Some even hide behind God. That's right, some women hide behind their beliefs or religiosity and make it all spiritual and never deal in the natural.

I want to encourage you to lose the mask you've been wearing by learning and releasing the 'Power of Forgiveness!' In order for you to move forward in your life and reach the purpose and plans God has ordained for you, let go of all that dead weight you have been carrying around from relationship to relationship. By letting go of your hurt, pain, anger, resentment and frustrations; you can experience a new lease on life. Forgiveness is the road to healing and the key that unlocks the door to your freedom. It is truly life changing!

Understanding Forgiveness

Letting go of hurt and pain caused by others can be very difficult because many people have a misguided point of view that if we forgive those who hurt us, it means we are condoning or excusing bad behavior? This kind of thinking causes some to develop a wounded heart that eventually leads to anger and resentment. Other people struggle with forgiveness because they want to forgive but they don't know how to or where to start. Allow me to help those of you who are struggling with forgiveness. First you must understand what forgiveness is and what it is not.

Through personal experience, I came to the realization that people get stuck forgiving others because they simply don't understand what forgiveness is. It's also difficult to forgive when we spend most of our time focusing on the offense. Naturally, we think if we forgive the person or people that hurt us it is sending the wrong message of condoning their ill behavior. That's so far from the truth. I discovered on my road to healing that forgiveness has nothing to do with the people who hurt me. Nor is it a sign of weakness like most people think.

Forgiveness does not minimize the wrong done nor does it deny the harm or the injustice produced. Forgiveness is not forgetting. It wouldn't be wise to forget the wrong that occurred because you can learn from your experiences. Most importantly, it allows you to set boundaries to help prevent the same things from happening again. If you forget a wrong, you are only suppressing feelings that can eventually turn into rage! Far too many times, people who suppress their feelings erupt like a volcano and take out their anger on unsuspecting individuals.

Finally, forgiveness is not losing. The mindset of forgiving someone is "losing" will cause you to stay stuck in unforgiveness. So get rid of that mentality and win in your life by forgiving.

Now that you have a general understanding of 'what forgiveness is not,' let me explain what forgiveness is. According to YourDictionary.com – "forgiveness" is defined as letting go of past grudges or lingering anger against a person or persons. This definition gives you a good understanding based on worldly principals. However, from my perspective, to truly know the power of forgiveness, one must understand it according to the Word of God. The Bible paints a clear picture of what forgiveness is and why it's important to our Heavenly Father. Forgiveness is a commandment and one of the primary reasons I believe people find it difficult to 'let go' of the hurt and pain caused by others. Many chose to forgive based on their emotions which is a costly mistake since forgiveness has nothing to do with how we feel. Thus, the reason God commands us to forgive if we want to be forgiven. He knows those ill feelings can lead us down a dark path of turmoil and a life span of emotional unhealthy behaviors with daunting side-effects.

The Side-Effects of Unforgiveness

Harboring negative emotions like anger and hatred can be detrimental to your overall health. These ill feelings can distort your view to a point of not realizing your attitude and overall behavior have been altered. You spend so much time pointing the finger at everyone else, you become a prisoner without realizing it. This is the reason I believe unforgiveness can be a silent killer. It's like drinking poison, but expecting the other person to die. This is how negative emotions "begin to take root in your heart" because you haven't taken ownership of your behavior and/or admitted that you have issues. Now you are experiencing the side-effects of unforgiveness unaware! There are three primary areas affected in our lives when we have an unforgiving spirit including emotional, physical and spiritual side-effects.

Emotional Side-Effects

The poison fruit of unforgiveness can be tied to our emotions which deal with our state of mind and overall behavior. I know from personal experience how anger can cause you to become very explosive! When you are emotionally wounded, you are typically driven by your pain and resentment toward others. Therefore, it's important to understand the source of your pain. If not, those wounds can cause physical harm to your body.

Physical Side-Effects

Not only does unforgiveness affect you emotionally, it can cause physical side effects including cancer and is classified in medical books as a disease. Studies reveal that sixty-one percent of all cancer patients have forgiveness issues and more than half are severe according to Dr. Michael Barry. He is a pastor and the author of "The Forgiveness Project: The Startling Discovery of How to Overcome Cancer, Find Health, and Achieve Peace." In his book, Dr. Barry shares stories of six cancer patients treated at the Cancer Treatment Centers of America (CTCA). He also made it known that harboring negative emotions, like anger and hatred, predictably creates a state of chronic anxiety which produces excess adrenaline and cortisol that deplete the production of natural killer cells that aid the body's fight against cancer. Dr. Barry's research included the study of our physical health, the relationship between the spirit of unforgiveness and cancer, as well as the relationship between forgiveness and healing.

Spiritual Side-Effects

I believe the spiritual side-effects of unforgiveness can have the most profound effect on us. Refusal to forgive your brothers and sisters from your heart only causes you to me tormented by the lies, betrayal, and the pain you won't let go of. I know from personal experience what it's like to allow anger to subdue you when it's deeply rooted in your heart and the torment that comes from reliving the pain on a daily basis. I'm so grateful for my journey. It has taught me some of the life's greatest lessons. More importantly, it taught me that forgiveness is the key that unlocks the door to freedom including the road to healing and restoration. However, when the secrets once hidden in my marriage were exposed, I was deeply saddened so I begged God for a separation.

My Road to Healing

Facing the truth on my road to healing wasn't easy. During the time apart from husband, I thought all my hurt and pain would subside. But, I was in for a rude awakening! I needed to be alone so I had no one else to blame. It was time to start discovering the truth about myself. Yep, that wounded little girl inside of me was running things all those years without the woman Sandra even knowing. Having to face the truth and looking at the woman in the mirror, I knew it was time to surrender all my cares to God and all that poison deeply rooted inside of me. I had to be detoxed from all my broken promises and bad decisions that led to my past wounded and once contaminated heart condition. It was time to be placed on the potter's wheel so I could be transformed from the inside out. So I was led on the road to healing with God at the helm of it all. He designed a way of escape from all my hurt and pain, but I needed to be obedient and follow His instructions. He used a dear friend of mine who was equipped to not only handle my pain, but to walk alongside me while my destiny was being realized and shaped.

I did the work necessary to gain knowledge, wisdom, and understanding of my past issues. It was done by going to counseling with my husband and attending small group classes: "Betrayed Hearts" for women whose husbands committed adultery. "Grief Recovery" that helps you to identify the places in your life where you first develop the behaviors you now possess or once carried. "Healing The Mother Wounds" blew my mind because I learned so much about myself including my own mothering style. Let me not forget "Boundaries" because God knows we certainly need them and last but not least, "Healing The Father Wounds." That class allowed me to see the wounded little girl in action and the one who was leading me in so many directions because of her need for love and acceptance.

In fact, the power of forgiveness was released in my heart one evening during my betrayed heart's class. We were instructed to write a letter to our husbands. The exercise was designed to help us "let go" of the pain caused by their betrayal. We were instructed to tear-up our letters, throw them away and say "good bye!" The moment I began tearing up my letter, the atmosphere shifted as the Lord's presence filled the room and my heart felt lighter as if a heavy weight had been removed! There was not a dry eye in the room! As I said "good bye" to the pain caused by my husband's betrayal, I knew "the power of forgiveness" had been released in my heart! I could sense the presence of God letting me know that it was finished! That experience was so powerful that as I was driving home, I could hear a still small voice say, 'I put him in your life for you to save him. He needs to see my love through you. If I was faithful and just to answer your prayers to expose him, why wouldn't I be faithful and just to answer your prayers for his healing?'

That message was powerful and profound. In other words, I believed God was saying now that I have freed you from the bondage of sin, change your mindset and begin to shift your thinking! Start praying for your marriage and your husband differently. The two of you are one in God's eyes, which means I can have a positive impact to bring about change not only in my marriage, but in the lives of others around me. Since I have been healed, delivered, and transformed from the poison once deeply rooted inside of me; my heart's desire is to share my story in hopes it will help you on your road to healing and restoration. It's not going to be easy, but it will be worth the life experiences God is ready to show you so He can eventually use your story for His Glory and to further the kingdom.

In closing, many people struggle with their identity and purpose wondering why they were put on Earth. Like me, you too must go through trials and tribulation to identify the root cause(s) of your issue(s) to discover your God ordained purpose in life. More importantly, you must trust the Master's Hand knowing He will never leave your nor forsake you.

I hope what I've shared has resonated with your spirit man. And, it's my prayer that at the end of your journey you too will receive your breakthrough and healing!

Tips to Becoming Free from Unforgiveness:

Tip #1 Healing is a Choice.

First you must understand that forgiveness is not the same as healing. However, the choice to forgive opens up your heart to receive healing. We must purpose in our hearts that we are ready for change. But, you can't move forward until you make the choice to stop blaming others and take ownership for your behavior. Remember, forgiveness is the process of letting go of those ill feelings toward others and they don't go away overnight. There is work involved. If you are willing to make the sacrifice, you can forgive through God's love, mercy, and grace. God does not put more on you than you can bear. He just wants you to walk by faith and trust Him no matter what. Your present condition is designed to bring "awareness to your behavior." If you are walking in a state of denial, playing the blame game, or acting like a victim; then know God wants to heal you! However, you won't get better unless you start dealing in truth and make the choice to receive healing.

Tip #2 Self-Examination – A Time of Reflection.

One of the most essential things I learned on my road to healing was to take time to reflect. I like to refer to it as "self-examination." It is the process of looking inward at our hearts for out of it flow the issues of life. The word of God tells us in Proverbs 23:7 (KJV), 'For as he thinketh in his heart, so is he.' Since many of us struggle with our emotions, it's important to spend quiet time reflecting. This can aide in our quest to learn the root causes of our issues. If you only deal with them on a surface level, you will continue to go through the same cycles. Have you ever wondered why the same things keep happening to you? If so, have you opened your eyes to the truth or are you operating in unforgiveness and refusing to be healed from your pain?

In order to be healed, you can't treat the symptom or cover up your issues. You must pluck them up from the root so you can begin taking your power back! As long as you continue to blame others or turn a blind eye to your issues, you will remain stuck! You cannot continue to do the same things and expect different results. No one likes to admit his or her own behavior stinks. Thus, the reason we need accountability and tools in place to help us identify those character flaws that are obvious to others, but not to ourselves. It's being able to take a look at yourself in the mirror. This can be challenging because you may not always like what you see. However, this is where change begins! Change starts with you as you begin to take your eyes off others and focus on your own issues!

Tip #3 – Know that God Loves You.

When it's all said and done, I want you to know that God loves you no matter what! The Word tells us that nothing can separate us from the love of God. Check out the tools available, do the work, and receive your healing and deliverance if you struggle with unforgiveness in your heart.

Self-Examination

Self-examination is essential in your healing process. You cannot move forward until you begin to look in the mirror and take off the mask! Oftentimes, I asked the Lord to show me "Sandra" including the errors of my ways, how He sees me, and what I needed to let go of. Some of the things He showed me were not always pretty. Therefore, I continually asked Him to 'Create in me a clean heart, O God; and renew a right spirit within me.' (Psalms 51:10 - KJV) Simply put, you must examine what's in your heart. If you desire to truly grow from your experiences, you must continue to work on your issues. Below are some questions to help you on your road to healing.

1. What person and/or people have you given your power away to because of unforgiveness? Why is difficult to "let go"? Journal to help discover the root causes of your issues.

   _____
   _____
   _____
   _____

   Are you currently going through trials and tribulations? If so, how are you weathering the storm? Journal what you are experiencing and what you are learning about yourself.

   _____
   _____
   _____
   _____

   What are you doing to help change your situation? Are you focusing on the other person or are you focusing on your own issues? What work are you doing to become free?

   _____
   _____
   _____
   _____

Meet Eureka Turner-Patton

What are three words that best describe you?

Confident, Extraordinaire, Noble.

What is the biggest challenge you've ever faced in life?

The biggest challenge in life that I have had to face is knowing if there was any more story to my life after becoming a divorcee. I have realized that I still have unlimited ink in my pen that allows me to continue writing the chapters of my life.

Where do you find your P.O.W.E.R.?

I find my "POWER" through the peace of God, the omnipresence of God, through the perfect will of God, the eternal existence of God as well as through the reverence of God.

A Confident Woman

Author: Eureka Turner-Patton

Philippians 1:6 *'Being confident of this, that he who began a good work in you will carry it on to completion until the day of Christ Jesus.'*

A "Confident" woman is "Courageous", "Organized", "Not needy", "Fearless", "Intentional", "Determined", "Engaged", "Noble", and "Transparent." Even with all these traits, she knows that putting her confidence in anything or anyone other than God, is building a life on an unstable foundation. Our confidence should not be measured by our credentials or our net worth but by the faithfulness of God. Because God has truly been in our corner from the start. With each new level we experience in life we will need to express our boldness and confidence in our gifts and abilities He has given us. Oftentimes confident women can be seen as untouchable or even prideful, but that is not the case with all confident women. I am writing this chapter to speak to the confident moms as well as those who need a boost of confidence. No matter what you have experienced in your life, rebuilding your confidence will help you walk in the doors that God has prepared for you.

Now before I make this sound too easy, I do not want to give you the impression that a confident woman will not have her fair share of challenges in life. I have endured many heartaches and disappointments and can tell you many times I wanted to throw in the towel, but my confidence in God caused me to keep fighting even when I wanted to quit. Surviving my first marriage which ended in a divorce, and raising two sons as a single mother was something I had never expected to happen to me. But it did, and I had to find the strength to overcome it. Looking back even in those darkest moments, I could see the fire in my eyes, and I knew that where I was then, was not always where I would stay.

Are you ready to become the confident woman you were created to be? If you have ever struggled with your confidence you know how difficult it can be to remain in a constant state of confidence. The challenge with remaining confident is not allowing yourself to become intimidated by what life presents to you. When you have a dream and vision for your life, tapping into your confidence will give you the strength to keep going.

Often times when I speak to women, I tell the story of opening a "Massage Envy franchise," despite not having the experience of running a retail business, yet it has been successful thus far. The entire process was very intimidating. It required long hours of research, completing applications, submitting financials, and sharing private affairs with their corporate office. They left no stone unturned. Just when you thought you were complete; more information was required. Although I tried to remain positive throughout the process I often questioned if it was worth it. Needless to say, I kept pursuing the dream.

After successfully passing the first phases, a visit to the corporate office for an in-person interview was the next step. I can remember the preparation to meet with the corporate executives of the company as if it were yesterday. It was a sunny, cloudless, beautiful spring day and I remember feeling the most confident than I had felt in an awfully long time. It is something special when you go after your dreams, it makes you feel confident when you place your fears to the side. That day represented years in the making.

Courageous

The flight was scheduled for 7:00 am and I set my alarm clock the night before for 4:00 am, to allow me quiet time with God. Before a courageous woman takes a risk, she takes time to be still and meditates to center her mind. I dressed in my Elie Tahari boss style navy-blue skirt suit. I selected that suit because I felt it best represented the courage I embodied. I took one last glimpse of myself in the mirror before going out the door. I was looking good, smelling good and feeling good; clothed with confidence.

Initially at the beginning of this process, I had no idea I had that amount of courage stored up in me to make this business venture a reality. But courageous women do not think twice about choosing the path that is less traveled. Even though the process seemed a little frightening, I had the courage and willingness to proceed, and dove-in for the sake of leaving a legacy for my children and providing jobs in the kingdom. I once heard Dr. George Frazier say, 'You can read about swimming or watch a swimming video but, until you dive in the water you won't really learn how to swim.' It was hearing this that prompted the green light to take the leap of faith into the water. Courageous women don't mind sharing what they have learned to help sharpen other women in their journey. *Proverbs 27:17 'Iron sharpens iron.'*

'Man cannot discover new oceans unless he/she has the courage to lose sight of the shore.

Andre Gide

About two hours later, the plane landed. It was a turnaround trip, so there were no checked or carry-on bags. Being chauffeured from the airport by a member of the company's executive staff and driven to the corporate office felt very welcoming. The meetings started promptly at 9 am and there I sat in the room of executives. My confidence had earned me a seat at the table. I was privileged to meet the CEO who shared his vision for the company, all department heads that were in direct connection with building out a new location, and other potential franchisees from other parts of the country.

In less than 72 hours from returning from our "discovery day," I was given the awesome news, the franchise agreement was approved. One of the lessons I learned from the experience is, do not allow fear to keep you from your dreams and goals. Instead be courageous and have confidence in God. He will never stop a good work until it's complete.

OCD (Organized, Creative, Detail-Oriented)

A confident woman is OCD. Being organized, creative and detailed-oriented has been a part of me since I was a young girl. Growing up my bedroom was always neat and in order and my closet was organized. Each section was grouped by color and length and each section was colorized from light colors to dark colors. My shoes were neatly packed in the boxes they came in, in sections of casual or dressy, stacked on the shelves. This continued into my adulthood and organization was displayed in every room of my home. In the kitchen pantry, the can goods were all facing forward and grouped together. I remember my girlfriends constantly teasing saying, 'you have a little OCD in you.'

"I just like everything in its rightful place." Well, when it came to opening the business, my OCD came into play. My "Organized – Creative – Detail-oriented" skills were much needed for the buildout process. I had a daily planner, my google calendar, Excel spreadsheets, cell phone, laptop, iPad, etc. were all used to keep me in the loop and organized. I was communicating with the banker, architect, attorney, financial planner, general contractor, vendors, franchise corporate office, insurance companies, county permit office, landlord, etc. It took some serious organizing to keep all these moving parts together.

Being organized requires some delegating. Even when you like doing stuff yourself, "like I do," at some point you will need to delegate. Delegating frees you to accomplish tasks that only you can do and should do. At the business, my employees know how I like things being in order. The front counter and office are clutter-free, customers should be given the highest level of customer service and respect, and the atmosphere should be welcoming, relaxing, and friendly. From the front to back clean, dusted, and smelling like Eucalyptus, Lavender, or other aromatherapy scents. The business should "always" be presented well, not just sometimes. A confident woman knows how important presentation is. Even as I am speaking about my business, think of ways you can apply this to your personal life.

As you increase in your confidence you will apply the things necessary to help you to become more efficient. Being a mom, a business owner, a professional, or a woman working her purpose, requires a lot of juggling, but it can be done. We are in the day and age of working smarter, not harder. Electronics are huge benefactors in helping keep us organized. iPads, iPhones, laptops, and how the devices link up together, just makes life so much easier. Use them for your benefit and adjust to make your life easier. Apps are time savers and efficient ways of conducting business and life.

'Organizing is what you do before you do something, so that when you do it, it is not all mixed up.'

A.A. Milne

Not needy

A confident woman is not needy. Not needy does not mean she doesn't need anyone; it simply means she doesn't need constant recognition or affirmation because she knows herself very well and she holds a positive self-esteem. She's a woman who has a plan and purpose and will not lose track of it. I remember when I was thrown back into the dating scene after my first marriage. I began dating and after dating someone for a short period of time, I would tell my best friend, he's not the one for me. She would tell me; you did not give it enough time. 'Yes, I did.' You see, when you have been shown some things by God, it doesn't make good sense to go back down that road again. I knew exactly what type of partner I needed, to potentially become my spouse. It was not about his status, title, or money; it was about his heart and his spirit. I did not date a man I knew would not measure up to the standard of man "here on Earth" I wanted represented to my sons. I didn't let my need overshadow the needs of my sons. I was not only seeking a mate for me but also a father figure for my children. He had to meet both of those criteria, and most of all being a Christian. I was not afraid to tell the person I was dating these facts, because I did not want to waste my time nor theirs.

Being with a confident woman doesn't work for some men. Why? Because some men are more attracted to women who are needy. The need of the woman tends to give the man a boost to his ego. However, I know that some needy women only act needy to make the man she is dating feel good about himself. Well, I just prefer to be genuine in all I do. I may not need you for all things, but it doesn't change the fact that I love you all the time. Needing someone doesn't prove your love for them, nor does not needing someone prove your lack of love. The need of a human being is not a 24/7 gesture, needs arise when you are incapable of handling somethings on your own. This is how a confident woman operates, she asks for help if or when it is needed.

Being straight forward and not beating around the bush is a confident woman's mode of operation (MO). She is not rude nor disrespectful, she is generally straight to the point. This does not mean she is heartless or uncaring; it is her "let us handle business" attitude. One thing for sure, a confident woman, will always be honest and upfront with her thoughts and feelings. Having this mindset propels her forward to having the life that she has always dreamed of which allows her the platform to help other women. She will invest in her wellbeing to be a benefit to others' well-being. 'Empowered women, empower!' She creates her own excitement and electricity as well as, in the meantime she is encouraging and "EXcelevating Lives" of other women to follow.

'In your neediness you repel, in your completeness you attract.'

Abraham

Fearless

Fearless women are confident, they live their life to the fullest. It does not mean they don't have some fears, but the difference is, their fears do not stop them, and they do not hide from things or people that pose a challenge. If she sees that something may not be in her best interest, she doesn't hesitate to change her course. When I was dating my husband, the one thing that stood out initially about him was his consistent behavior and his intellectual conversations. He saw me for the strong and independent woman that I am, and we just have a mutual respect for one another's personality.

Being a fearless confident woman means you are willing to try even if you fail. Your fearlessness allows you to be resilient and bounce back from any situation in life. Can you think of any areas of your life where you could exhibit more fearlessness? I want to offer you encouragement to go after the things you deserve. I want to encourage you to see yourself as God sees you. Fearless women do not make excuses for their life choices. They accept the consequences both good and bad, and they learn the lessons necessary to make better decisions.

As a fearless woman, you are not concerned with what others are doing or accomplishing because you are more focused on what you're doing to advance your plans and purpose. Yet, the key is getting your tasks completed, as well as doing what you can to help and assist other women EXcelevate. Many times, we are fearful of other women outshining us when God has given each of us our own assignment. You don't have to go out of your way to prove you are fearfully and wonderfully made, it should be seen naturally. Even more so, a fearless woman should not have to hide her brilliance, because it makes another person uncomfortable.

'Do not shrink your beautiful light to make someone else feel more comfortable. Be who you are without hesitation and you will inspire others to shine, too!'

Intentional

Intentional living is a common thing for confident women. They don't just wake up and aimlessly go about their day. They have a planned agenda be it for home, business or personal. Living an intentional life requires knowing what you are living for, in other words, knowing your purpose. What are you passionate about that is above yourself? Write it down and make a plan for it to give meaning to your life. To live your life intentionally as well as on purpose takes necessary steps to accomplish, what you feel, think, and do. These steps will help provide *FLAGS* to navigate that will not only help you to survive but will also help you survive day-to-day as well as to thrive.

Here are the "FLAGS" to help you lay a foundation to live and thrive intentionally:

Focus

In this day of the internet, cell phones, computers and cable television we are bombarded with staying connected to people which tends to keep our attention from the things that require our focus. It is up to us to master detaching from the worldwide web and cable tv in order to live our intentional lives. As for me, I was not a big fan of Facebook or any other social media sites but, to get your message to the masses, it is needed. However, it can consume you if you let it. It's about having balance and setting a particular time of the day to communicate on social media.

Learn

Increase your knowledge, get a mentor/coach. Never stop learning and investing in yourself. Surround yourself with likeminded people and learn from them. I've always been intrigued with people who are game changers as well as being open to other information they are willing to share about their success. I did not let their success make me feel inferior or less than. Stay connected and learn, learn, learn.

Assess

Determine where you are and where you want to go. It will require you doing some reflecting to figure out if you should go left or go right. No matter what direction or path you take, it will need your undivided attention. Living intentional means, you have an intended purpose for how you go through life. Each day builds upon the next day, the next week, the next month and the next year. Take time to meditate and seek God's direction.

Goals

Without goals you will not know when you have accomplished anything. Goals give you a sense of achievement when you have completed something you had set out to do. Goals can be short-term, long-term or both. Set SMART goals that are Specific, Measurable, Attainable, Relevant and Timed.

Survey

Take a survey of yourself to determine your strong and weak skill sets. This will let you know where you will need help in accomplishing your plan and purpose. Although, God has given us all we need to fulfill our purpose. We cannot do everything; we aren't good at everything. For example, if math and numbers is your weakness, then you may need to seek out an accountant or bookkeeper for your business.

'The power of intention is the power to manifest, to create, to live a life of unlimited abundance, and to attract into your life the right people at the right moments.'

Wayne Dyer

Determined

A confident woman is determined. When she is focused on completing a task, she does not allow anyone, nor any difficulties to stop her. She understands that determination is a valued asset to help her get to where she wants to go in life. Determination is a crucial component of being successful in achieving goals in life, which means not giving up when things get too hard. You can count on having some failures and disappointments along the path of success, but determination keeps you going in spite of. Success is generally not an easy win. Keeping these practices in mind these will help you remain as well as be more determined.

Refrain from Complaining, Criticizing, or Whining

'Spending today complaining about yesterday won't make tomorrow any better.'

Anonymous

Complaining, criticizing, or whining about a problem or situation is a waste of time because it doesn't correct what's wrong. Instead use the time to find a solution.

Consider the people you spend your time with. Limit your interactions with negative people who constantly whine, you will start picking up those traits. I know you've heard the saying, 'Misery loves company' and it's true. So, think seriously about replacing those relationships with ones who are more positive and supportive.

Don't Stress Over Things You Can't Control

"Take life day by day and be grateful for the little things.

Don't get caught up in what you can't control. Accept it and make the best of it."

Mancandangel

You cannot control people or situations, but you can definitely control yourself. In many cases, if we can only change our expectations of people, it could possibly reduce negative feelings that result from experiencing unmet expectations. Therefore, it would benefit us to direct our attention to ourselves as soon as we realize we are getting annoyed with someone else.

Write down your thoughts to help you manage and understand them better and realize that the things you cannot control are less important than you think.

Relax your mind with morning meditations and inject a sense of peace and gratefulness around the things you can control and lessen your focus on the things you cannot.

Be thankful for the daily blessings and celebrate what you have and have accomplished and not pay much attention to what others have or have accomplished.

Engaged

Confident women understand the importance of being socially engaged. It enhances our wellbeing as well as those we engage. Engagement requires being present and listening to others. When we make others feel special it softens them to be more engaging. Remember, it's not about you, it's about them. If we live with that kind of mindset, we all would be better at constructive and positive engagement.

In business, a confident woman engages others for feedback and insight, she knows she doesn't have all of the answers. Therefore, she embraces her team or circle of influence to brainstorm on certain topics and/or situations. She shares her vision to engage her team on the endless possibilities that can arise from it and gets their buy-in to generate cohesiveness and excitement.

Women with confidence engage and take the time to acknowledge and appreciate her team of partners because they took part in her vision and she will do the same for them, if or when they choose to pursue their own vision. She doesn't try to hold them hostage in her own vision and retaliate when they want to chase their dreams. They supported her; therefore, it is only right for her to support them.

'When you engage in fulfilling the needs of others, your own needs are fulfilled as a by-product.'

Dalai Lama XIV

Noble

Noble is a word that refers to people of royalty. Confident women are of royalty, we all are, it is in our DNA. Yet, confident women are royal because of their fine qualities, high moral principles, and honorable ideals. Her style, mannerism and behavior set her apart. She's rare, noticed, and valued.

On a Sunday morning leaving church, it happened to be Easter Sunday, we were driving around looking for a location for our franchise. We drove by a piece of land with a sign saying, "Target coming soon." I immediately sent an email to the corporate office asking if that area met the criteria for the franchise. A few days later, we were informed that the area qualified. The franchise location is named "Aliana" which means "Noble and Gracious." When I realized the meaning of the name, I knew we were led to that location. We opened our franchise there because it totally represents who I am as a person and in the fashion, I intended the business to operate in. A confident woman is also gracious, courteous, kind, and pleasant.

'To express gratitude is gracious and honorable, to enact gratitude is generous and noble, but to live with gratitude ever in our hearts is a touch of heaven.'

Thomas S. Monson

Transparent

Confident women are seen as women who are transparent and trustworthy. They are open about who they are, where they are, and what they are. Transparency opens the way for a more respectful relationship with others. Withholding the truth about yourself doesn't help you, it actually limits you. It limits the fact of allowing you to be real with yourself and others. Those who are confident in their skin know that their faults or failures are not judged by others because they know God is the only one who is qualified to judge. No one is without faults and should not be throwing stones. 1 Samuel 16:7 But the LORD said to Samuel, 'Do not consider his appearance or his height, for I have rejected him. The LORD does not look at the things people look at. People look at the outward appearance, but the LORD looks at the heart.' When we are emotionally mature, we can be emotionally transparent about ourselves which conveys transformation from within.

When I was a young girl, I grew up very sheltered which made me very naïve about life and relating with people my age. I attended Catholic schools from kindergarten to junior high school in Louisiana. So, when I relocated to Houston, I started attending public schools for the first time in the 6th grade which was a rude awakening. I didn't know how to relate and stayed to myself. Why? Because I was afraid of being transparent of letting others know I was so behind the eight ball than they were. The conversations the girls were having, I could not participate in because I had not been in any of those situations. They conversed about dating and having boyfriends and I was clueless to it all. I stayed to myself and remained disconnected to cover the realization of not knowing or experiencing any of the topics being discussed. I had finished high school before I really was able to allow myself the freedom of being transparent. Because of that, I missed out on the fun activities a student should enjoy and embrace during those years. Nonetheless, I finally caught up with life in my twenties. I don't regret being sheltered because I know it was done to protect me and for my own good.

> 'Transparency produces trust, and trust is the foundation that manifests authentic relationships.'

I would like to encourage you to find your voice and exude your confidence. Remember, there was a time when I lacked confidence because I did not know that I had the confidence that I needed until I built a relationship with God, cultivated with like-minded women and I associated myself with impactful spheres of influence. I patterned myself after positive role models. No matter where you are in life you can find the confidence you need to go the next level. It may seems challenging at first but if you use the tools that was presented in this chapter as a template you can face the world of uncertainty and thrive.

Meet Shannon Gooden

What are three words that best describe you?

Confident, Ambitious, Passionate.

What is the biggest challenge you've ever faced in life?

The biggest challenge I have ever faced was accepting help. I was fiercely independent and thought it was a sign of weakness to ask for or accept help. It made me feel like I did not have the ability to succeed on my own. I was used to facing life completely independent, not having to rely on others. Ironically, it was easy to give help, but hard to receive. Mostly because I became accustomed to people coming to me for help and advice. People saw strength in me and drew from that strength. But admittedly, I was not strong enough to reach out to others for help for myself.

Where do you find your P.O.W.E.R.?

I find my "POWER" in God. God has given me the strength to conquer and overcome my obstacles. Being a woman and mother with power, has allowed me to empower and influence other women to find their inter-power.

Shift Your Mindset to Abundance

Author: Shannon Gooden

At the age of 16 I knew I was different…unique. I grew up around small-minded people who put themselves in a box, but I wanted to go out far beyond the box and explore life. I fell in love with numbers and wanted someday to become an entrepreneur and help people find their financial breakthrough, after growing-up around so much poverty. I saw life through a different lens from those around me. I always seemed odd to those who thought my dreams and aspirations were just a fairytale. Giving, and touching people through my experiences, expertise and knowledge, while helping to change the lives of people, was far from a fairy tale – it was my truth and something God put in me. What I did not realize, is along the way I would face giants.

Being a young girl, life was simple, but after becoming an adult, it became challenging. After graduating and receiving my degree in finance, all that I had dreamed and envisioned, it was now time to conquer and live out those dreams. I got married at the age of 22, right after graduation and later became a mother. As the years progressed my career grew but my marriage did not. I felt my spouse became intimidated and jealous of my success and became resentful rather than supportive, which was one of the reasons that led to my divorce.

After my divorce, life took a major turn for me after becoming a single mother. Trying to manage my career and still impact others, became extremely difficult. *How could I find the time to balance it all and accomplish my goals?* I wondered. I began to question my purpose and if I would ever fulfill it after transitioning into this new phase of my life. I found myself at a crossroads and felt like I was forced to give up on my purpose, serving and helping others achieve financial abundance. The faith and drive I once had was becoming a thing of the past, until I began to surround myself around people who empowered and motivated me to accomplish my goals despite my challenges.

My Outlook Changed

A few years back, I attended a business conference that changed my outlook on my finances and future. I was surrounded in a room full of other young leaders who were looking to take their career to the next level and create a legacy of financial wealth for their families. Amongst us were several successful entrepreneurs. These individuals have already taken the initiative and have built a successful business and have created long term wealth for their families.

At the conference each speaker taught about the fundamentals of a business and how to create wealth from a financial perspective. But If you are anything like me, I like to dig a little deeper into things and first focus on the "why" and the "what" versus the "how". I became interested in learning about the root cause of why people lack financial freedom. Researching the "why" would then help me to identify the problem, that would then allow for me to help myself as well as others achieve financial freedom. I started with using the Bible as a resource. I then dived into psychology looking at people's financial behavior and experiences, which lead to my interest in financial mindset.

Growing up, I have always had a sense of curiosity. I had an urge to analyze and figure things out. Most people thought I would have become a detective, lawyer, or maybe even a psychologist; which honesty I thought about each one of those careers, but instead I became interested in accounting and financial management; therefore, I became an accountant and financial coach.

In my career, I have worked for some of the largest corporations and I have learned a lot about budgeting and financial management and what it takes to become financially free. Majority of us struggle with managing our finances mostly because we do not have the right mindset and we lack financial literacy. After being in my career almost ten years now, I have learned that true success and freedom starts in the mind and having a healthy relationship with your money.

Even the most successful people still have trouble with budgeting and managing their finances. Some may have already accomplished financial freedom and wealth, but they have an unhealthy relationship with their money. Have you ever heard the saying, 'Don't Let Money Control You, You Control It'? Well, let's just say money holds the power in most of our lives. We have become enslaved to it and we want to spend, spend and spend, becoming undisciplined and putting us in debt rather than freeing us from it. Although I am financially literate when it comes to money, I too struggled with excessive spending while going through my separation. Everyone has a different way they handle stress, and for me it was shopping. Shopping was therapeutic and temporarily relieved the stress, until one day guilt set in, and I decided to take control back over my finances.

Shifting Your Mindset

When I began to study my Bible and read what God says about money and how we are to use it, my mindset and perception of money changed. Not only did my spending habits change, but how I viewed money and where I placed it changed. I realized that money was connected to God and that He was my source, so I studied how to get financial abundance through Him.

In life, our mindset determines the road we will travel on. Whether it is a road paved in scarcity or a road full of abundance, the decisions we make today, greatly impact our finances in the future. Through research and experience, I have discovered the reason why we have trouble managing our finances or obtaining financial freedom, ultimately comes down to our mindset. Everything starts in the mind, so why not start there. I was once told we cannot fix a problem until we get to the root cause of it. The root is the foundation and if our foundation is not solid, what is built upon it will collapse or die. Think of an apple tree. In order for a tree to grow it must be properly rooted and it requires water and sunlight to produce good fruit. Just like our mind we must continue to feed it with knowledge in order to grow. The moment we stop supplying the nutrients our mind needs to flourish, we become stagnant.

As I approached this chapter, I began to think about the different mindsets people face when building their financial story. Although there are several mindsets one could face, these are the most common mindsets: Scarcity Mindset, Consumer Mindset, and a Fixed Mindset.

Scarcity Mindset

Some of you may have experienced a scarcity mindset at a time in your lives whether it was in your childhood or adult life, where your mind told you there was not enough, in return you experienced a shortage in your finances. Scarcity means "the state of being scarce or in short supply; shortage". I remember growing up and being around several people with this mindset. Due to their circumstances and environment they saw limited opportunities, resources, and wealth. They experienced a lot of doubt and believed there was a limited amount of money. With having this mindset, it is impossible to achieve financial freedom.

Consumer Mindset

On the contrary, you also have people who take on a consumer mindset. When you think of a consumer, you're probably wondering aren't we all consumers and without consumers, businesses would not exist. Yes, you're right, but what happens when the consumer becomes excessive in their spending and lands them in debt? A consumer mindset feels the need to always buy things even when they do not need it. Having a consumer mindset is the most common mindset and lands a lot of people in debt.

I fell into this category. Shopping was almost like a drug, something easy to start, but hard to stop. Admittedly, shopping has always been a hobby of mine, but not to the extent where I could not control myself or I would feel an adrenaline rush. After intentional introspection I discovered I was suppressing my feelings and instead of dealing with the problem, I threw money at it. I was ashamed to call myself an accountant and not to mention a financial coach because it was a contradiction to my profession. How could I help someone else and I couldn't help myself? How did I let my emotions spin out of control and allow my lust for shopping to trump my knowledge of financial management? Instead of saving money I would spend it.

Does this mindset hinder you from achieving financial freedom? Instead of budgeting your money do you spend it shopping on other unnecessary things? Or do you just simply have no idea what to do with your money? Being a consumer is not a bad thing, but if what you are consuming consumes you, this is where the problem begins.

Fixed Mindset

A "Fixed Mindset" is the most critical mindset because people are content with their financial situation. This mindset makes people believe that there is nothing wrong with how they spend their money. They are not looking toward the future, but they are looking at right now. With this mindset it is hard to persuade a person to change their behavior or think about long-term wealth because they have an unchanged mindset.

There are people who have the financial knowledge, but instead they go contrary to what they know until they are in a financial crisis, or they are faced with retirement. What you do now determines what your future will look like. With these types of mindsets, we must shift it to think beyond our circumstances and our environment. Some things that we were taught growing up, we must unlearn those things, and those things we were not taught we must learn. Our behavior toward money must change in order to achieve financial freedom. We all desire to become financially mature in our spending and eventually become financially free, so now we must learn what it takes to achieve that desire, by faith and disciple.

Some people never think about faith and finances being in the same sentence, mostly because we do not truly know what money is and what we are to do with it. We only look at money to buy material things. If you look in the Bible God speaks a lot about money and how we are to use it. God promised to meet every need, so why do we have a scarcity mentality? Or why do we feel we have to spend every time we get money? The Bible instructs us to get wisdom in all things, that also includes our finances. This goes for those who are rich and those who are not rich. Those who are rich also struggle with their finances due to a lack of discipline and having an unhealthy relationship with their money. Being educated does not mean you have wisdom. Also being rich does not mean you have wisdom, that is why rich people also need financial guidance because of their mindset.

After discovering the three mindsets that hinder us from financial freedom, you're probably wondering what type of mindset I must develop to achieve financial freedom. Three mindsets we must develop in order to become financially free, is a Growth Mindset, Business Mindset, and an Abundance Mindset.

Growth Mindset

A growth mindset is having the desire to learn and to improve. This is the first step to achieving anything, we must first decide and set goals. I like to call it a "hungry mindset". I became hungry enough to seek knowledge in the things I wanted. Are you hungry for more? Are you ready to achieve your goals you have set out to achieve? Well, all it takes is a willingness to change. Studies show that the number one fear in America is public speaking, but I would disagree and say "change" is the number one fear, and change is what breaks barriers.

Once we are willing to change, we can then start to shift our mind to thinking on a business level and developing our business mindset. Businesses cannot grow on its own, and neither can your finances without proper strategies and discipline.

When it comes to money you do not have to be an accountant to be an expert in managing your finances, but you should have a business mindset. No, you do not have to go to college to achieve it, like anything it takes someone to teach you, a mind to receive it, and a heart to believe it. Most of us who are not accountants or have a financial background, do not look at our finances as a business, they look at it as a personal tangible object. Like a business seeks to grow and multiply, we must also seek to grow and multiply our personal finances.

Business Mindset

Let's start thinking about our finances from a business standpoint. Instead of spending it, let's develop goals and strategies to multiply it. With this mindset we will always make decisions looking into our future to make sure we have stability and long-term growth. Now we are ready to step into our Abundance Mindset.

Abundance Mindset

This mindset is my favorite because this is where you have taken all limits off and realized that anything is possible through hard work and faith. At this point you are unstoppable. An abundance mindset believes there is plenty of everything to go around. They are very optimistic and positive in their thinking. They are not greedy nor selfish. They believe in faith and are not fearful. I love this mindset because you are in full control outside of God. Society does not play a role in your life or decisions. You are confident and are truly happy with your life because you have the faith that you will succeed. Abundance does not necessarily mean money and wealth, but simply being happy and confident in your life and future. This does not come overnight, but we are shifting our mindset to think abundance and wealth and be disciplined in our spending now and enjoy our fruits later.

Money is a gift from God, and He entrusted us with that gift. He wants us to seek wisdom to live a life of wealth and prosperity. Instead we worship money and that is what puts us in debt. Although I am an accountant, I too had to shift my mindset. I learned that not only did I need financial literacy, but I also needed faith and wisdom. Once I realized what money was for and that it was connected to God, I started to take better care of it, not because I worshipped money or that it became my god, but because it was God's and how I treat Him, I also treat what belongs to Him.

We must develop a disciple mindset after we have transformed our mind, to eliminate the toxic thoughts and behaviors toward money. We want a new approach and an open mind for good seeds to be deposited. Change your thought process. You do not have to make decisions on your own, let God be your resource. Obedience is the key component in this transformation of your mindset. Be confident in your decisions and trust the process.

Now that we know the first step toward financial freedom which is creating a money mindset, let's explore how to "level up" your finances through budgeting and financial management. Financial management becomes easy after you have learned the root cause behind the struggle of financial management. It's like a puzzle, once you find all the key components in the puzzle, you can then start piecing them together. Since we have received the first puzzle which is mindset, we are ready to explore the second piece of the puzzle which is financial literacy and budgeting.

"Level up" your Finances

Managing your finances is something everyone must do, whether you have one dollar or ten billion dollars. Nothing states that you must have a lot of money in order to manage it, however, people take on that thinking. Becoming wealthy does not come overnight, unless you win the lottery or come into an inheritance. Unfortunately, neither one of those happened for me and if it had, I still must manage it in order to keep it and learn how to increase it. It all comes down to disciple and control.

Being a single mother pursuing my career and becoming an entrepreneur, I sometimes find it quite difficult to sit down to plan and manage my finances. I am busy wearing multiple hats, that I sometimes lose track. As we know nothing goes exactly how we plan it, but planning is necessary. It keeps us on track and helps us become proactive rather than reactive. When you know why you're planning and budgeting, it becomes a lot easier. Having a reason is motivation to pursue financial goals. My son is my reason, and I know that every dollar I save, every budget I set, and every paycheck I manage, I am setting up his future. Do you feel like you don't have time to budget on a consistent basis? Do you give up when trying to budget? These are all normal human behaviors when it comes to finances, but it doesn't have to be that way, that's why I share my knowledge with you to encourage you to level up your finances through the process of budgeting, saving, and investing, so you can have financial freedom and live the life you desire.

Well, let's start with the first step which is budget planning. Planning is the key component to financial management. Financial planning helps you to determine your short and long-term financial goals and creates a plan to help meet those goals. Just like building a house, you must have a blueprint. Think of your finances like building a house, the house represents your goal. First you need to clearly plan out and budget from your income. Budgeting your income helps you determine how much money you will need for your expenditures such as tax payments, monthly expenses, and savings.

Budget planning helps you to know where your money will be spent. Knowing where your money is going gives you control. You must be consistent and precise in your planning so you can then begin properly budgeting and managing. I am big on setting goals because it gives you something to strive toward. I found that it is harder to manage your finances when you do not have goals. I believe everyone has a goal. We must all strive to increase our funds and create generational wealth. I also discovered that for some it is easy to make money, but it is difficult to keep it.

Creating a budget sheet is simple. We know that in any budget you will have fixed and variable expenses. These expenses will always be a part of your budget. Although they may fluctuate in amount, we can never get rid of them. Make sure to incorporate any debt into your budget and include any savings.

Why is financial planning important? Financial planning with the help of a financial expert will help you reach your financial goals. Here are eight reasons why financial planning is important:

- ***Income***: Managing your income helps you to know how much money you will need for your expenditures.

- ***Cash Flow***: Increase your cash flow by monitoring your spending patterns and expenses.

- ***Capital***: An increase in cash flow can lead to an increase in capital.

- ***Investment***: A proper financial plan opens the door for investing into your future.

- ***Assets***: The planning process helps you build assets.

- ***Financial Literacy***: Better financial understanding helps you to achieve financial goals.

- ***Family Security***: Providing financial stability for your family.

- ***Saving***: Save discretionary income to create long-term stability.

After budget planning and finding out why we need to plan, our second step would be to save. Saving is the door to financial freedom. We make decisions about our money every day, but we never think about saving our money for the future. You may have to start small and create a solid spending plan, this will allow you to know where your money is going and to eliminate waste.

Now let's start with some general saving ideas to get you "Thinking Like A Saver". There are several ways to save and several reasons to save. You can also have several saving accounts for different savings. Here are three saving tips:

- ***Create an Emergency Fund***: Creating an emergency fund is a must. Having an emergency fund gives you flexibility if something unexpected was to occur. The amount of money one must have in their emergency savings account may vary depending on the person, but I would recommend having at least 6 to 12 months of expenses in your account. This money is only to be used in case of an emergency and not for your future savings.

- ***Retirement Savings***: Retirement is a top priority for those who are savers and should be for everyone. Start early to build wealth long-term. These savings should never be touched until retirement. Continue to grow and increase your retirement until you are ready to retire. This plan is outside of your 401K.

- ***College Savings***: If you have children, saving for college is also a top priority. Investing in a 529 college plan will help you achieve your college saving goals.

Building Financial Freedom & Creating Generational Wealth

Creating wealth may sound impossible to some, but it is possible if you are willing to create it. But how do you obtain financial freedom and generational wealth? You invest smart, build wealth, retire early, and live free. This is a blueprint to building wealth and becoming financially free. Building wealth is not easy nor is it quick, but it is realistic and attainable with the help from a financial expert and strategic planning.

What does it mean to "invest smart"? Investing smart simply means to know how and what to invest in that will get a good rate of return on your money. Whether it is investing in stocks, bonds, mutual funds or real estate, investing in retirement is important in your financial freedom. You can invest at any age, but it is best to invest at an early age because younger people have something older people do not have, and that is time. What you invest today determines when and how much money you will have to retire. Most people invest between 5-10 percent into their retirement, but did you know that investing around 15 percent can get you to retirement and financial freedom faster? The more you invest, the more money you will have. That sounds simple right? Well it is, however, investing into the market can also be risky, that's why you should seek a financial advisor for guidance on what funds to invest in. Real estate is also a good asset to invest in and to pass down to future generations. Creating multiple streams of income is the way to build your wealth. Start by increasing your current income and then start adding multiple streams of income. Invest your money every single day even if it is just five dollars.

How do most people retire early or become wealthy?

Becoming wealthy does not fall in most people's laps, you must create it. Some people think it is impossible, and some think it cannot happen for them, but anything is possible if you choose to believe and go after it. There can be barriers in becoming wealthy without the proper understanding. Some people do not have the proper resources or have access to knowledgeable people to help guide them, but that is no excuse. There are many materials, books and online resources to help you no matter what stage you begin investing.

Personally, I wanted to know how so I sought out people who had what I wanted. I remember a couple of years back reading Robert Kiyosaki's "Rich Dad, Poor Dad" book as well as "Business in the 21st Century" and it changed my outlook on how to create wealth. I grew up thinking wealth came from having a great career that paid six figures, but I soon realized that was not true. Don't get me wrong making six figures is great, but how long will that last? When will someone pull the cord or maybe demote you? Or what happens when you become tired of working that job? Where is the asset you built? I learned that working for yourself was the best way to go. Yes, working for yourself also has its own challenges, but at least you are building and creating something that can be passed down to the next generation and you are building wealth. Robert talked about how the economy is not stabled and we cannot depend on it, and he talked about how to be mentored by someone who has what you want.

He became wealthy by following behind and observing the man who he wanted to become, his "mentor". He taught him what and how to do certain things. With any business you want to increase revenue, but how can you increase it? One way is doing what the brilliant Ray Crock, founder of "McDonalds" did, and that was duplicating his business and collecting a percentage of each store's revenue. Ray Crock has over forty million stores around the world. This is what creating a legacy and generational wealth looks like.

Our goal in life is to make a difference and leave a legacy for the next generation as generations before us have done. Teach your children and the younger generation what it means to save and manage their money and why it is important. Incorporate in their everyday life money management skills. Today is the perfect time for them to start to invest in their future. Teach them that it is not all about money but teach them that it's about making a difference in the world and other generations. As for me learning how to become financially literate and learning money management skills, put me in this position now to make a difference in someone else's life and finances, and encourage them to teach their children and the younger generations as well. God has equipped each of us with different things to share with the world, so I share this with you all. It is never too late or early to educate our children. We want to make sure they start early investing and be ready to face the world with certainty and wisdom in all things, including their finances. Let's teach them that they can and will change the world.

It is time that we take control of our finances and live a life of abundance that God speaks about. Together we can change the world and live how we are designed to live. With the renewing of our mind, proper guidance and resources on our finances, we all can reach financial freedom and create a life of wealth and abundance. God said, 'I came that they may have "life" and may have it more abundantly.' John 10:10

I encourage each of you to change your money mindset and create a profitable path and start taking control of your future. As a single mother I have faced many situations and have jumped over many hurdles, but I continue to stay focused and trust God that he will guide my footsteps as well as yours. To all my entrepreneur moms; keep the faith and continue the journey on creating a life of true wealth and abundance, and I pray that I have given you more wisdom in your finances and created a desired heart to make a difference in your finances and others.

It's Time For You to Tap Into Your POWER

We have reached the end of our time together. Do you feel encouraged and inspired to push through and rewrite your story? Each POWER Mom expressed her life lessons through her lenses, and she held nothing back with the hope that her transparency would encourage you to embrace your wings and soar. We are passing the baton to you, and I want you to reflect on what your life story has included that can inspire the next woman.

As we conclude of our journey today, this is where I leave you with your marching orders.

The last letter of POWER is "R" and it stands for Restore. Maybe you have felt lost and that no one understands you. Maybe you feel as if you have lost your voice. Or maybe if feels as if everyone has turned that back on you and you are all alone. You are not alone. Jesus tells us He will never leave us or forsake us, so you are never alone, but there is more. He also knew that you would need people to love on you and restore you. This is what I pray this book has done and will continue to do after you close it. We all have scars that we carry around with us, but we must allow the healing to take place. This is the beginning of our restoration.

Are you ready for your total healing- mind, body and soul? If you have not done so already, go ahead and forgive yourself and the people that have hurt you. After you have done that write out your vision for your life. Pray and ask God to direct you to the people that will help support you on your journey with their prayers and sound wisdom. After you have written the vision start seeing yourself with a fresh and new perspective and start taking action. Finally, apply the lessons you have learned from this book to help direct you in your divine purpose and elevation.

Let me prophesy this to you. This is the year that you will see God move for you like never before. This is the time you will see the areas that were once broken in your life, become restored and made whole. This is the time you will experience your greatest comeback story. It's never too late for you to live out your purpose and tap into your POWER. This time it will work out for you! Do you believe it? There's no more time to procrastinate or make excuses. Your time is now! Go forth and remember there are more for you than against you. I can't wait to read you story next.

I love you and I am praying for you---It's Go Time!

Blessings,

Dr. Sherrie Walton

To connect with me visit: www.iamsherriwalton.com or email admin@iamsherriewalton.com

To join the POWER Moms movement visit: www.powermomsbook.com

About the Power Moms

Dr. Sherrie Walton

Her Excellency, Rev. Dr. Sherrie Walton, is a United Nations Ambassador at Large, Guest Lecturer, Keynote Speaker, Author, Global Entrepreneur, University Lecturer, Film Producer, Publisher, and "Mompreneur" Mogul. Dr. Sherrie is the founder of Sherrie Walton Consulting and Walton Publishing House where she helps women birth their "book dreams" and creates compilation books and platforms for women speakers, business owners, and everyday women with stories of empowerment. Sherrie is the founder and creator of the Mommy & Me Dream Bigger Tour; an International multi-city (2) day experience that teaches moms and kids how to overcome their fears, pursue their dreams and reshape their lives. Dr. Sherrie is a licensed minister and is the Co-Founder of Wildfire Ministries, and partners with her husband as a Spiritual and Life Coach to NBA Players with Family First Sports Firm. In addition, she is a marriage coach and has been married to Dr. Christopher Walton for 18 years. Together they have 3 beautiful children, Christopher II age 12, Kai-Milan age 9 and Winter age 7. She is the program consultant for Big Sister Little Sister for 9 universities in the U.S. Sherrie has been seen on ABC News, Fox News, CEO Mom, and various media outlets.

Kineta Lewis-Harrison

Kineta learned the funeral industry from some of the best leaders around. She's a devoted wife and doting mother of three. Kineta has been in the industry at premiere locations in Houston for 20 years, promoted to general manager, recognized for excellent service, management and leadership; awarded "Essence in Leadership" & "Manager of the Year", served as a corporate trainer, certified celebrant, public speaker and panelist. Kineta is connected with local non-profits, Grace Kids, the Legacy Team, East Aldine, Baker Ripley, Green Bayou Coalition, NAMI Greater Houston because of her passion for loss prevention through Suicide Awareness and a proud graduate of the UH SURE program. She continues to lead by example, comforting the brokenhearted and celebrating the lives of the departed. Kineta is a dynamic leader who ensures the success of her team.

Araceli Avionn

Araceli earned her Bachelor of Science Degree in Technology Logistics and Supply Chain Management from the University of Houston, a Master of Business Administration from The Institute of Florida Technology and a Certification of Professional in Human Resources from HR Certification Institute. Araceli has a successful track record in leading and developing professionals in management while building a career in logistics management. Araceli is the proud mom of a seven-year-old son. Araceli enjoys exciting and inspiring future leaders. Her love and passion for leading, teaching and mentoring helped to guide her to a path of following her dream of becoming an Adjunct Professor for the University of Houston Downtown.

Dr. Linda Bell-Robinson

Dr. Robinson graduated from Educational Leadership Doctoral Program at Sam Houston State University. She received her Master and Bachelor of Arts degrees from Texas Southern University. She attended Texas A & M, Texas Woman's University and Sam Houston State University through the Leadership Command College and is a former President of the Leadership Command Alumni Association. Dr. Linda Bell Robinson brings 36-years and retired as a Lieutenant investigator with the Harris County District Attorney's Office Asset

Forfeiture Division through-out her professional career, has been appointed to several local and state commissions. In 2003, she was appointed by Governor Rick Perry to serve as a member of the Council on Sex Offender Treatment. In December 2004, she was selected by the Governor to move to the Council on Health and Human Services, where she is an active member. In 2013 she received the Outstanding Texan award from the Texas Legislative Black Caucus. A community servant, Dr. Robinson is the elected Precinct 0104 Chairperson for her community.

Alessi Johnson

Alessi obtained her Bachelor of Arts degree in Broadcast Communication, from the University of Louisiana at Lafayette. While in college, Alessi was awarded after ranking number one as the "Best Radio Journalist in the South," by the Southeast Journalism Conference in 2011. In 2012, Alessi graduated as Summa Cum Laude of her graduating class. She was recognized as an Outstanding Senior in the Department of Liberal Arts for her work and study in Broadcast Communications. Shortly after graduating, Alessi landed a job in radio working as an On-Air Radio Personality for KNEK Magic 104.7, which broadcasts throughout Southwest Louisiana. Often referred to as an "Old Soul," Alessi became the youngest African-American female to grace the airwaves of an Urban Radio format geared towards a demographic of listeners ages 30 years or older at the age of 23. In Alessi's work in Social Services, she has been recognized for her accomplishments as an "Outstanding Mentor" for serving at-risk youth in the Greater Dallas/Fort Worth area.

Nkia Haughton

Nkia's life is truly a testament of triumph amid adversities. From day one of her life she had to fight for survival after being born at just six months in gestation. A chain of unfortunate events included being in a car wreck and losing her ability to speak with seizure episodes, molested and raped, physically abused, suicide attempt, verbally abused, and rejected for the most part of her life. To date there are no residuals of her life experiences for this she gives thanks to God. Nkia has studied at Molloy College. She is also a Sure Graduate a (subsidiary of the University of Houston). She is a military spouse and a mother of one son.

Sandra Heard

Sandra is a visionary, forward leader. She is a powerful, thought provoking author, coach, motivational/inspirational speaker, and spiritual guidance advisor. She holds a Master's degree in Business Administration with a concentration in Accounting from DeVry University Keller Graduate School of Management and a Bachelor of Business Administration in Finance from Cleveland State University. Sandra is the founder and president of Speak Life Ministries and she is also a co-founder of Akron Summit Scribes Faith Based Writer's Club. She works with her husband as a pre-marital mentor, and counsels couples whose marriages are in need of healing. Sandra Heard is married to her best friend James and is a mother of three and has two grandchildren. She is a humble servant of our Lord and Savior Jesus Christ! She is passionate about sharing the Gospel and the good news that Jesus Christ lives; she desires to bring healing to the wounded souls and broken hearted.

Eureka Turner-Patton

Patton was named 2019 Top Black Professional & Entrepreneur of Texas, 2019 Top 30 Influential Woman of Houston, 2019 Woman of Excellence by the Federation of Houston Professional Women, and 2019 Mrs. Texas in the Mr. & Mrs. Black America Pageant (MMBA) or which she was the Third Winner-Up. Patton is the 2020-2021 National Ambassador for the Ms. Mr. Mrs. & Mr. Black America Pageant and December 2020, she will graduate from the Chayil International University with an Associate Degree in Leadership, Business & Ministry. This highly proficient and successful business powerhouse has adopted as her motto the expression, "Eureka... I found it!" because she is constantly looking towards new discoveries and business opportunities that will propel her to elevated levels of success. In July 2018, she opened the doors to her own company, Massage Envy – Aliana. In her free time, Eureka enjoys traveling, sports – especially football, and listening to jazz. She's a mother of two sons.

Shannon Gooden

Shannon Gooden is an accountant and Certified Financial Coach with 10 years of experience. She studied at the University of Missouri – Kansas City where she earned a Bachelor of Business Administration in Finance. Her passion is to help break the cycle of financial bondage and to create a mindset to help conquer financial fears. Her goal is to empower and educate people to make the best financial decisions and to achieve financial independence. Outside of the office she dedicates her time conducting financial management classes and workshops around her community. With her knowledge and expertise, she wants to help change the world and current financial situations. She is the proud mom of one son.

Additional books in the P.O.W.E.R. Mom Book Series

Volume I- P.O.W.E.R. Moms, 12 Stories of Moms that Found their Power to Win

Volume II- P.O.W.E.R. Single Moms: Persevere. Overcome. Win. Empower. Restore

P.O.W.E.R. Moms books are available at Barnes and Nobles, Books a Million, Amazon, Walmart and wherever books are sold.

To order bulk copies for your church, organization, women's group, or book club email: thepowermoms@gmail.com

The P.O.W.E.R. Moms are available for speaking engagements, podcasts interviews, radio interviews, blog interviews, television interviews and magazine interviews in the United States and abroad.

To book the P.O.W.E.R. Moms email: thepowermoms@gmail.com

To tell your story in the next P.O.W.E.R. Moms book volume email: admin@iamsherriewalton.com

www.ingramcontent.com/pod-product-compliance
Lightning Source LLC
Chambersburg PA
CBHW071418070526
44578CB00003B/598